This book is for you, if you.

- come from a foreign country and do not speak good English;
- are lonely and hurting;
- are broken-hearted;
- are a widow or widower;
- are very successful;
- think you can never become successful; and
- have lost your loved ones.

This book is written for everyone;
a believer and a non-believer,
for family, husband, wife and child.

1

What people are saying about Leila...

"I know many sons would say this about their mother, but truly I am one of the most blessed sons in the world to have a mother like mine."

Jacky Jean Wilks (JJ), England

"Leila is a woman of phenomenal strength ... she puts into place the foundations of a legacy ... "

Bishop Otis V. Wilks, stepson, Hemel Hempstead, England

"My sister Leila is a very compassionate person and family-oriented ... always likes to help and give to other people. When it comes to life storms, she is very strong."

Jennelisa Casenares, Leila's younger sister, Cagayan de Oro City, Philippines

"She is brave, strong and has wisdom and principles in life, which she lives by."

Jorge Pao, Leila's third brother, Cagayan de Oro City, Philippines

"She is a very kind-hearted person, who never complains ... She has been through many struggles in life, but they have helped her become who she is today as such a wonderful person."

Nellie Busano, Leila's elder sister, Cagayan de Oro City, Philippines

"My Aunty Leila, to me, is the greatest person in the world who I know. She is one of a kind and one in a million. I appreciate all the advice she has given to me, I take it in with much gratitude."

Alnel Dagohoy, one of Leila's nieces, Cagayan de Oro City, Philippines

"Leila is small in stature, but large in fortitude!"

Pastor Brian Boggis, South Hill Church, Hemel Hempstead, England

"... my first impressions of Leila were – as a woman of few spoken words, with calm demeanour yet strong, a respectful wife, a caring mother, a straightforward, yet sincere person, a friend and always a hard-working person ... The more I came to know her, the more I knew how strong she was, steadfast and a sacrificial woman for the sake of family."

Glorecita-Omac-labadan (Glory Tan)

"Many people have been blessed by her prayers and friendship, as well as her smiling face! She is an amazing person and she has an amazing story!"

Nigel and Marion Coleman, Hemel Hempstead, England

"When I was approached by Leila about joining a women's group, at first I was a bit apprehensive, but then having listened to what God had instilled in Leila's heart, my apprehension was put to rest. Having attended the meetings, there is no doubt that God's purpose is being unfolded in each member of that group."

Rocquel Wright, Saint Albans, England

"She is a fighter, a strong woman and a warrior. She always puts God first; that is why impossible things become possible to her and she knows that God is always with her."

Katrin Camelle Busano, KC, Cagayan de Oro City, Philippines

I have always found Leila to be very hospitable, pleasant, loyal, well mannered, extremely hard-working and always willing to give a helping hand and advice wherever possible. I have never known Leila to lose her cool, nor seen her angry at any time. She has a caring heart for helping children and people in need and loves them as much as she loves herself. She is mentally strong and I have known her to handle difficult and hard situations she has encountered. She has loved through thick and thin, sickness and health, poverty and wealth."

Yvonne Thompson

"Leila Wilks is a very special lady ... Her persistent, encouragement, good personality and influence has contributed to our success today. Leila's built strong relationships and took good care of her family, using her strong personal values. We learnt a lot from her about how to enlighten and encourage other people. Her story and experience will definitely help many people who want an extraordinary life! Thank you for what you have done in our life, Leila."

Jason and Wanfui Zheng

"Leila is a true friend, good sister, a loving mother to JJ and, most of all, a wonderful wife to Ven. She is also a very generous and kind-hearted person, and I admire her family too."

Helen Wallis, Jasaan Cagayan de Oro City, Philippines

"Leila has a big heart for people in all walks of life. She has a strength and determination to follow God at all times and has overcome so many obstacles to do this. She does so with wisdom and knowledge of God's word. To know Leila is a blessing and privilege, and I treasure her words of wisdom in my life."

Joanne Rowell

"Leila, a willing servant of Christ Jesus. Willing to be transformed to make an impact on lives for His Kingdom. Leila, you have been such a blessing to my family and me. And with your book, so many more lives will be transformed for His Glory."

Michelle Attoh, Hemel Hempstead, England

"I got to know the real Leila when our lives collided during a women's conference we attended in Leeds. She is on fire for God, always encouraging and uplifting anyone who will allow her to minister to them. Leila has a genuine heart for people because she shares her life experiences with God. I am confident this book will change your world."

Abiola Bankole, Hemel Hempstead, England

"Leila is like a big sister to me. She is calm, patient, kind and easy to talk to. I have learnt so much from her on my spiritual walk. Leila is positive, an excellent role model and a teacher. She has a spiritual gift of evangelising other people. Leila was the person God used to contact me, to share the formation of the Women's Support Group (WSG). I love Leila so much."

Alison Graham, Hemel Hempstead, England

"Leila, you have been a wonderful witness of what our most High God can do with obedience and trust. Your heart cry is to trust and obey as there is no other way to be happy in Jesus but to trust and obey. This is the song of your life as His humble servant. Leila, you are also a fervent prayer warrior with a commitment to see hearts saved and lives restored for Jesus. You are a faithful leader of the women support in our church enabling sharing of testimonies and the study of the word for growth and encouragement of all. You are His prized possession and it is such a privilege to know you, dear Sister Leila. May you remain humble and seek only His perfect will. Amen!"

Tina Louise Khan, Hemel Hempstead, England

"I met Leila in South Hill Church, Hemel Hempstead in 2012. Since then, God has been using her mightily in my life. She is a powerful woman of God with a child's heart and a beautiful faith."

Sandra Satler, Hemel Hempstead, England

"From the first time I met the late Venroy and Leila, I felt an instant connection. They both had a beautiful smile. Leila appeared very coy, but her smile radiated. Ven, on the other hand, was quite the opposite, very confident and relaxed. I felt as though I had known this couple for some time. Today, that very coy Leila, by the grace of God, has blossomed into a very confident, self-assured individual and has taken up where Ven has left off. Although we don't get to see each other as much as we would like to, due to life's inevitable challenges, our special friendship and faith keeps us together. Leila knows that she has a special place in my heart, together with her wonderful son JJ, who has developed into a very enchanting individual, overcoming many obstacles over the years."

Jennifer Holder, London, England

"Leila is a very dear friend, with a passion and zest for sharing the good news of the Lord Jesus Christ. We have known Leila for four years and during this time, we have become close friends seeking to share the gospel, while also supporting and nurturing other Christians. Leila lives out her faith on a daily basis; loving the lost; praying for the needy; and truly living by faith. Leila has been instrumental in generating opportunities for women in our local area to meet and share fellowship together; and she is an inspiration to many people in our church and community. Leila's sole life purpose is to serve the Lord in all she does and to share her faith with as many people as possible, every single day."

Ross and Claire Crawley, Hemel Hempstead, England

"She is a remarkable woman, who is like a spiritual Mum to me ... I thank God for her in my life."

Kelly Marie Dolling, England

"A doting, loving and proud mother, who has instilled honour and the merits of hard work, through focused achievement to her lovely son, JJ. Although Leila has suffered great loss and hardship in her past, she has risen through the mire, with grace and an untiring conviction in her heart, to overcome her trials. The perfect example of a hard-working lady, with warmth of human spirit and the resilience of her good character shown in the best light during adversity. Leila is open, caring and compassionate, with a refreshing zest for anything she puts her mind to. She places the comfort of other people as an earnest endeavour, where she tirelessly supports family and friends near and far. The sentences I have used above to describe Leila are limited in intimating the actual essence of the lady I am honoured to know."

Dorothy Worburton, London, England

To read the testimonials in full,
please see Leila's website
www.leilawilks.com

About Leila

Leila grew up on a farm and lived an ordinary life with her parents and siblings in the Philippines. When her mother was diagnosed with bone cancer and diabetes, she stopped going to school and looked after her mother. When she was 14, she made a terrible mistake and had to run away from home. Leila married Venroy Wilks and moved to England, which was a struggle as she did not speak good English. Together with her husband, she set up a business venture as well as managing day jobs. They did everything they could to provide for their son, Jacky Jean, JJ. They worked hard, trying their best as most parents do. Little did they know, however, that they were putting too much effort in one area of their lives and neglecting other areas, which are also important, and had battles and disasters to face coming around the corner, including a strong typhoon.

Leila's book will take you on a journey of her life and the many stormy seas she survived. Her book will open your eyes to events you may never have seen before in your life, which may have contributed to your sufferings. You will discover how crucial it is to balance important life values, which Leila calls the 5 Fs.

These are: Faith; Family; Finance; Fitness; and Friends.

Leila's book demonstrates that when you have too much of one value dominating your life and very little of the others, you will feel empty. You will only have balance in your life and feel at peace and in a place of love when you live your true life purpose aligned with these five values.

There are no disasters, only opportunities

You raise me up

A true story of loss, love and hope, resilience and faith

Leila Pao Wilks

Published by Filament Publishing Ltd
16 Croydon Road, Beddington, Croydon,
Surrey, CR0 4PA, United Kingdom.
+44(0)20 8688 2598
www.filamentpublishing.com

ISBN 978-1-911425-76-2

© Leila Pao Wilks 2017

The right of Leila Pao Wilks to be identified
as the author of this work has been asserted
by her in accordance with the
Designs and Copyrights Act 1988.

All rights reserved.
No part of this work may be copied without the
prior written permission of the publishers.

Contents

Foreword	13
Chapter 1 – The Philippines; a simple, rural childhood	15
Chapter 2 – The Philippines; Ven arrives in my life, in an envelope	28
Chapter 3 – The Philippines; marriage and motherhood	35
Chapter 4 – London; life, death, family and personal challenges	43
Chapter 5 – London; the rat race, from cleaner to business owner	53
Chapter 6 – London; personal growth and a flourishing business	61
Chapter 7 – London, Jamaica and the Philippines; family travels	71
Chapter 8 – The Philippines; a new life and new challenges	79
Chapter 9 – The Philippines; goats, pigs and public transport	91
Chapter 10 – The Philippines; dealing with unknown demons	103
Chapter 11 – The Philippines; health and financial disasters	111
Chapter 12 – The Philippines; healers, helpers and hospitals	121
Chapter 13 – The Philippines; hope shines brightly in the darkness	131
Chapter 14 – The Philippines; debt, dialysis and more disasters	139
Chapter 15 – The Philippines; spirits, miracles, Typhoon Sendong	149
Chapter 16 – The Philippines to London; Ven goes home at last	161
Chapter 17 – London; reality, relatives and reading	167

Chapter 18 – Hemel Hempstead; a life purpose at last   177
Notes, Definitions & References   187
Leila's Five Life Principles   189
Acknowledgements   193

Foreword

For the last two decades, Leila has immersed herself within a world of positivity. This consisted of mental programming acquired by reading the correct books and listening to audios whilst attending seminars and associating with like-minded people. Leila understood early on that a positive mindset would enable her to achieve those things previously beyond her reach. She realised early on, when you rubbed shoulders with successful people some of their success rubs off on you.

Leila developed her own strategy for success known as the Five Fs: Faith; Family; Finance; Fitness; and Friends. Leila developed a holistic approach to her life that allowed her to work in harmony and remain focused whatever storms she weathered. Therefore, this allowed her to strengthen and build herself up. Once you have read her life story, you will realise: *'tough times never last, but tough people do'*.

Her story will inspire you, while taking you on a roller coaster ride of emotions. Leila has a story to share that will undoubtedly change lives forever.

Paula and Roger Galloway

You raise me up by Leila Wilks

Chapter 1 - The Philippines; a simple, rural childhood

I am one of eight siblings from my father Luis and mother Georgia. We called them Papa and Mama. I am the second eldest sister after Nellie and before Jennelisa, Abel, Joe Marie, Jorge and Joel. We have a half-sister called Enesia, from Papa's first wife who died during childbirth. Eight years later, Papa married Mama, and they were blessed with seven healthy children. Mama Georgia came from the mountains, from Kalakaran Manoligao Carmen Agusan Del Norte in the Philippines. She owned a small grocery store in Barrio Manoligao where we lived, as well as a piece of land she inherited from her parents in Kalakaran, which Papa cultivated. He also bought and sold chicken eggs. Mama's store was a success, and I have many happy memories from that early time of my childhood, where I was surrounded by natural love and genuine happiness. However, when I was nine years old, Papa and Mama decided to close down the store and we moved to Kalakaran in the mountains. They built a little home for us there on the quarter acre we owned, and Papa stopped selling eggs and focused on making the farm productive.

My sister Nellie and I went to school in Manoligao, near the market. We walked every day, five days a week, and it took us 40 minutes each way. I remember when I joined the daily flag ceremonies, I was always at the front because I was the shortest pupil. I was worried and nervous because when we sang the national anthem, I felt uneasy. I sweated and felt as if I was going to fall over. I had to work hard not to fall, by shifting my position, but this was a problem I never told anyone about. This only happened during flag ceremonies and I intentionally came to school late to miss it and go straight to class instead. I never understood why I was like that.

You raise me up by Leila Wilks

We lived off the land and from what we caught in the nearby rivers; small fish and shrimps mostly. Our lunch was always boiled cornmeal with roast salt fish, which we wrapped in banana leaves. We opened them up and ate them with our hands under the shade of a big tree in front of the school.

Every year, we experienced typhoons when we were unable to go to school because of the danger of flooding. I remember a particular typhoon from my childhood, which washed away most of the crops in our area. We planted sweet potato and the day after the typhoon, our backyard was scattered with hundreds of potatoes and cassava. We picked them up and bagged them. Thankfully, they lasted us for weeks and we felt blessed for all that food after the storm. We didn't have shoes in those days and walked barefoot. We carried everything on our heads, which is probably why we never grew in height! We could not afford to buy rice. It was a luxury for our family, but we loved to eat boiled rice and sometimes, when we had a good harvest, Papa treated us. I remember I had a habit of hiding a few kilos of rice and later, when we really craved it, I took it out and cooked it for us to share. Papa would wink at me as if to say I'm a clever girl... he he!

We were very poor but we didn't know it, because for us it was simply our life; it was normality. However, we owned a carabao, a big, black, cow-type animal with two horns, which I enjoyed riding.

In those happy childhood days, we all worked on the land and, at five o'clock in the morning, my father woke us up and prepared a hot drink for us before we went to the farm to help cultivate it and clear the weeds. It was not an exciting life for children but we had nothing else to do and no toys to play with. Papa, who was a hard-working man and focused on what he was doing, didn't say much, but I learnt many life skills from him and from the land he taught us to cultivate. One morning, I was lying down

Chapter 1 - The Philippines; a simple, rural childhood

on the ground looking up at the sky with my sister Nellie and an airplane flew very high over us. I said to myself, "I am sure somebody is flying that machine and there are people inside it. One day, I will travel in one of those and I will look down at the world and see everything below me." We were ignorant about vehicles in those days and had never heard an engine, only the machines in the sky above us!

When I was five years old, there was a big fight between the rebels who lived in the mountains and the military under the Marcos Government*. The rebels, who were opposed to the Marcos laws, attacked the local military camps built by the army in the country areas. There were horrible killings between these people, as well as many innocent civilians. We were accused of giving the rebels support and had to stay in the Barangay Captain's* home. We couldn't sleep because we did not feel safe. It was a very frightening experience for young children, and scary for the adults as well. We heard guns firing continually during the night and day. We also heard that some of our neighbours were killed and we were told not to say anything. Papa decided to take us to Alicomohan where he came from. As soon as the shooting had stopped early one morning, we packed our few belongings and walked to Carmen to catch the bus to Papa's place. Most of us who lived in the mountains sold our goods and left the place, but because we left our farms, the rebels took our crops and they stayed in our homes. However, we had to leave otherwise we would all be killed. We got to Papa's place and very quickly built a small house with the help of our relatives there. My sister Nellie, our younger sister Jennelisa and I went to Alicomohan Elementary School. When we were not at school, we worked with Papa to harvest coconuts and processed them to sell. We also helped him make and sell charcoal. It was our single means to an end. Papa also planted banana and cassava around the coconut farm, which we looked after. After Nellie finished year six, she went to High School in Papa's town in Sugbongcogon, Misamis Oriental and I joined her there later on.

17

During the two years we lived in Alicomohan, we went through many horrendous storms. I remember once, we saw big coconut trees breaking and falling down so we looked around for coconuts and collected them to sell. I liked living in Alicomohan because we were surrounded by Papa's family and relatives, and living there was good for us plus we were close to our granny, Papa's Mama. She took us to church every Sunday and told us memorable things such as, "God is coming very soon and the world will come to an end." I used to think to myself there was no point in going to school and finishing my studies if the world would be ending soon.

In 1975, when I was 13 years old, we heard the trouble back in the mountains in Kalakaran had settled down and Papa decided we needed to go back and look after the farm we had there. He sold our small home in Alicomohan, though we were not keen on going back to the mountains. We had enjoyed living in the town, where there were more people and cars on the road. We lived near the main road and for the first time in our lives, we were exposed to a wider variety of people and machinery. We had made friends with our cousins and we got to know all our relatives in the area. However, Papa and the rest of our family went back home to Kalakaran in the mountains, while Nellie and I continued to go to Sugbongcogon High School, under the supervision of Uncle Isabelo and Aunty Linda, which made us happy and sad at the same time.

When I was 12, Mama Georgia developed an illness in her bones. After a year, she was diagnosed with bone cancer and also Type 1 Diabetes. Nellie and I decided to leave our school in Sugbongcogon and join the family. We moved to a secondary school in another town closer to Carmen. Mama had a cousin who lived there and she offered for us to stay in their home. They had a big rice plantation around their home and sometimes we stayed there at the weekend when they were harvesting. We earned money by selling our harvest and we took rice home with

Chapter 1 - The Philippines; a simple, rural childhood

us. I loved to eat rice because it was much tastier than cornmeal. Nellie and I learnt how to cultivate rice farms by working with my aunty and cousins. They paid us every time we worked for them. Papa and Mama were pleased because they did not need to give us money to buy our school uniforms and accessories and we took provisions home too. Although rice farming and corn farming both required hard work, one big difference was the rice farming was on a thick muddy soil most of the time. We had to wear boots and sometimes there were scary creatures who crawled on our skin and stuck to our legs. They also sucked our blood, which was horrible and it scared us.

Eventually, Mama was diagnosed with cancer. Mama Georgia had to see the doctor quite often and Papa decided to rent a small house in Carmen so Mama didn't have to walk far for each of her appointments. The doctor did not have a cure for her cancer and advised us to take her to the seaside, where she could stay in the water every morning. We moved into a little house by the sea but Papa still worked on our farm from Monday to Friday and came home at the weekends. I stopped going to school to look after Mama Georgia. We talked together about everything, and I was the closest child to my mother. Most of my relatives said I looked very much like my mother and I believe I did. Mama told me, "Do unto others what you want others to do unto you." At the time, I did not have a clue that these words were from the Bible.

Mama was a very patient, quiet person and very kind to everyone. She had a character of not wanting to upset people and I was the same. Mama said to me, "Whatever happens in life, there will always be someone there to guide and help you. Always pray to God." I remember Mama's mother had forced us to kneel down and pray every night when she was with us. She used to pick on me because I was quiet and never complained. She asked me to lead the rosary and I became devoted to praying with her.

You raise me up by Leila Wilks

My sister Nellie had moved in with our relatives in Carmen and continued her studies there. She liked to dance and she became a popular dancer in her school. I was in Carmen with Mama, together with my brothers Jorge and Joel. Papa looked after the rest of the children with him in the mountains. Every morning, I took Mama and my two brothers to the sea and she always enjoyed it.

Nellie was doing well with her dancing, and Granny Anastacia financially supported her studies by selling green bananas. One day, Nellie invited me to go with her to Uncle Democrito's home in the mountains of Kabalawan. They had a dance event every Saturday night and Nellie's first boyfriend came from there. I really enjoyed watching my sister dance, wishing I could do the same. She was very good at it. I stood in the corner and watched her and said to the people around me, "She is my sister." I was very proud of her and everyone there loved her.

One weekend, Papa's harvest was ready at the same time that there were many thieves stealing farmer's harvests. It was a very common thing to happen in those days and everyone watched their stock carefully. Papa asked me to stay in our house in the mountain with our dog, while he stayed with Mama that weekend. Nellie came in the afternoon on the Saturday and invited me to go to a dance with her to a place near where Uncle Democrito lived, which meant we could sleep in my uncle's house that night and leave our harvest with the dog to guard. However, I was reluctant to go because I knew how important it was to have someone in the house. I told my sister how important it was to watch the stock we had, but she insisted and said one night wouldn't do any harm. She said she was sure it would be fine. We would come back early the following morning and she said the thieves were busy stealing stock from other houses, not ours. Eventually, I decided to go with her to the dance.

Chapter 1 - The Philippines; a simple, rural childhood

We had a great night and a lot of fun with our cousins and the rest of the family. The next day, after having our breakfast, we started our journey home to our mountain farm. When we were near home, there was a strange feeling inside me. My heart was pounding. We saw our neighbours across the river before we reached home and as soon as they saw us, they looked very worried. They ran towards me and firmly warned me to not to continue walking towards our home. We asked what had happened. They told us that our father was violently angry with me because, when he arrived in the morning, he found out that no one was in the house and all of our harvest was gone! The thieves had stolen it. They said Papa was screaming, calling my name and saying, "Come home, Leila! I want to kill you!"

I was very scared, but I insisted on seeing my father to explain. However, Nellie ran first to see my father and to explain to him that it was her fault. I followed her, but as soon as he saw us approaching, he ignored her and ran straight towards me with a big knife, ready to chop me up. Granny Tasing, Anastacia, was there and she ran and stood in front of me, protecting and covering me and shouting, "Run, Leila! Run!"

My father pushed my granny aside and faced me. In his anger, he accidentally dropped the knife, but he beat me up instead. I was in so much pain; he beat me up badly. My granny got up and did everything to stop him, but eventually I slipped his grasp and I ran as fast as I could. I went to my neighbour's house where they quickly put me inside their bedroom and hid me there. I heard my father's voice shouting for me, then he stopped and asked our neighbours, "Where did she go?"

They pointed towards the town and Papa left calling my name, with the knife in his hand. I was very weak and bruised. I did not know what to do. My neighbours told me to go as far as I could so that Papa would not see me. My sister and Granny did not know I was there. I decided to go back to Uncle Democrito's

21

house. I was crying all the way. It was a very sad experience for a 14-year-old girl. I was very weak, confused and scared. I had been looking after my mother for more than a year since she was moved to live in Carmen and I started to really miss her. It was a very sad thought for me to realise I could not go there now, because Papa wanted to kill me. Uncle Democrito and Aunty Estelita were puzzled to see me back. I nearly collapsed when I arrived on their doorstep. I explained everything to them. Uncle was very angry with my father.

He said, "If your father comes here, I will beat him up!"

He was very concerned that Papa will come and look for me there. Uncle came up with the idea of taking me back to Alicomohan, where we had stayed when we had fled from the rebels. The next day, he decided to take me there to Uncle Isabelo, Papa's brother, so I could stay in his house, because at least there were many of them to protect me, if Papa found me. I felt very sad though and I kept thinking about my mother. I was very worried that the news of what had happened might make her illness worse. I missed her very much and I wanted to explain the facts to her, so she would understand. I knew she would listen to me.

But instead, the next day, Uncle Democrito and I caught the bus to Alicomohan. It was a two-hour bus journey and I grew sadder and sadder because I was getting further and further away from Mama. When we arrived in Alicomohan, Uncle Isabelo and Aunty Linda were shocked when they learnt about what had happened. Uncle Isabelo and Aunty Linda promised to take care of me and swore to fight with Papa if he tried to harm me. The next day, Uncle Democrito left to go back to his home. I did not stop crying. I was very sad, scared and very hurt. He hugged me and reassured me that he and Aunty Estelita will come and visit me. I felt very lonely and confused after he left. I was very scared that Papa would come and find me and that he would kill me. I told Uncle Isabelo and Aunty Linda how scared I was. They understood that sooner or later Papa would come and find me so decided to take me even further away to Cagayan de Oro City to one of my other aunties. Papa did not know where she lived in Cagayan. Uncle Isabelo was going to take me there the next day. That night, I did not sleep.

I cried and cried, and Mama was my great concern. I cried myself to sleep, and in my sleep, I dreamt about my mother. She was wearing a long white dress. I was standing beside her at the seaside and Mama was talking to me.

She said, "I want you to look after all your brothers and your sister Jennelisa. Promise me not to get married until your brothers are old enough to look after themselves."

I said, "Yes, Mama, I promise."

But I had to ask her in that dream, "Why are you asking me this, Ma?"

She said, "I am going somewhere far away."

"But I want to go with you," I said.

"No," she said, "you cannot come with me. Focus on looking after your sister and brothers."

Suddenly, in my dream she slowly faded up into the air waving her hands, and said, "Don't forget your promise."

I cried and called her name, but she slowly disappeared.

I woke up crying.

The next morning, I got myself ready to go with Uncle Isabelo to the City of Cagayan to live with one of my aunts there. I was sitting on the balcony when I saw one of my granny's cousins from Carmen coming towards the house. I was shocked to see her. She rushed into the house and said to me, "You need to go back home to Carmen with me. Your mother died."

I stood there… I was shocked to hear this and I cried more profusely!

I said to her, "Please tell me you are not serious," and I told her about the dream I had the night before! She explained what had happened leading up to her death on January 24th 1976 at five o'clock in the morning.

When Papa arrived in Carmen and looked for me, he told Mama Georgia what I had done and what had happened to our harvest. When Mama heard the bad news, she cried and begged Papa to look for me and not to hurt me. She begged him to bring me home and to forgive me. She said to him, "We will be fine. We will be able to find food to eat." But Papa did not listen to her and continued to express his anger towards me. Mama kept crying. She asked her relatives to look for me. She said to Papa that I was only a 14-year-old girl and I must be very scared, confused and feel abandoned. Mama understood what I was going through, as I knew she would, but early the next day, she died. My granny said she died with tears running down her cheeks.

Mama's death made Papa even madder at me. He blamed me for her death. Several of the neighbours and relatives blamed me as well. It was an extremely shocking and painful experience for me. I had looked after my mother for nearly two years and now she was gone. I didn't even have a chance to see her or say goodbye.

After her death, my burden, my promise to my mother – the road to Calvary – got worse. Instead of going with Uncle Isabelo to Cagayan, I went with Granny Pelomena back to Carmen. Papa's family had sent money and food to help him, and Uncle Isabelo

Chapter 1 - The Philippines; a simple, rural childhood

and the family was on my side and tried to comfort me. I cried on the bus all the way on the journey and people on the bus were asking my granny what was wrong with me. When she told them I had lost my mother, they felt sorry for me.

The day I travelled back to Carmen was my mother's funeral. They did not keep her long. I was desperate to see my mother's body, but Granny Pelomena was very worried that Papa would kill me if he saw me. She warned me not to go near my father. It was a very unfortunate journey for us because the bus we were in was delayed by a couple of hours and when we arrived in Carmen, they had already buried my mother.

I was so intensely hurt. It was a very painful feeling to know I did not see my mother's coffin. I was angry and devastated. I went to look for my father. This time, I did not care about what he wanted to do to me. I felt in my heart he was the one to blame for my mother's death! I ran towards our small home, and my cousins and Granny Anastacia and Granny Pelomena tried to stop me. But I was determined to see my father. When the relatives saw how angry and mad I was, they went to my father to guard him. I screamed at him! Calling my father's name! He was angry and I was angry! Everyone tried to stop both of us getting near each other. I shouted and screamed, expressing my feelings and blaming him for what had happened. My father was desperate to come near me and beat me up.

I shouted at him, "I am not afraid to die! Kill me if you want!" But there were many people there to stop him.

Granny Anastacia took me to the cemetery and I knelt down at my mother's grave, and remembered what she said in my dream: "Look after your brothers and sister."

My relatives told me that after the funeral, Papa tried to commit suicide but they stopped him. One of my uncles told me what happened during the funeral. He said Nellie was very hurt and disturbed and blamed herself for everything. When they were about to take the coffin down, Nellie screamed and asked them to bury her instead of Mama and one relative, who was annoyed with her, pushed her towards the hole, but somebody grabbed her before she fell in.

After that, my sister Jennelisa and brother Abel told me what happened on the day Mama died. Papa sent them to let Uncle Democrito know that Mama had passed away. Jennelisa was 11 and Abel was nine years old. The two children walked alone all the way from Carmen to Kabalawan, my uncle's place, which was a long way from Carmen and a very mountainous walk. They told me it was raining heavily and they were soaking wet, but they had to continue. When they reached Kabalawan, they found the river was very high from all the rain and it seemed impossible for them to cross. Both of them sat on the ground and cried because they were afraid the current was too strong and they could not see anyone there to help them. Suddenly, an old man came towards them and asked if they wanted to cross the river. They were very pleased and told the old man what had happened. He led them by the hand across the dangerous river and then he disappeared. They did not know where he went but they ran all the rest of the way to Uncle Democrito's home and told him what happened.

The agony of losing Mama in such a terrifying way was very painful. I remembered the days when I had got up at three o'clock in the morning to prepare porridge for her and sit and watch her eating it. I remember to this day how it hurt me so much to see how skinny she had become. After her porridge, she went back to bed and I woke her again at five o'clock to take her to the seaside with Jorge and Joel.

After the funeral, our family completed a 40-day prayer process, during which Papa tried a few times to kill himself, but fortunately

Chapter 1 - The Philippines; a simple, rural childhood

there was always someone there to stop him and remind him his children needed him. Papa's anger towards me slowly melted.

After the 40 days of prayer, Papa decided to take Jennelisa and my brothers home to the mountain of Kalakaran. Nellie stayed in Carmen to finish high school in the Academy and I went back to Sugbongcogon to continue my second year of high school. When I completed my schooling, I started working immediately and sent as much money home to my father as I could to help with my siblings' education and fulfil my promise to my mother. I learnt not to dwell on the past and to stand up for myself. I worked firstly in Aunty Adelfa's store and afterwards as a childminder for several families. I then worked in a Chinese restaurant, a seaweed cleaning factory, sold charcoal stoves, and later concentrated orange juice, door-to-door, and also worked in a rum company. Eventually, I moved to Cebu and worked in a pizza café before I became a store manager in a photography shop. I was happy at last: I had a place to live; I earned good money to send home and I made new friendships. I fell in love, learnt to drink beer, smoke cigarettes and listen to music.

By the time I was 27 years old, Joel had finished high school and he joined me in Cebu, where at last I had my four brothers living with me and working. One night, I realised how my promise to my mother in my dream was now completely fulfilled. I was very happy to know I had really done it! They were with me now, but living their own lives and I was being looked after by my brothers. I felt like a princess!

You raise me up by Leila Wilks

My mother (on the left) at my brother Abel's christening

Chapter 2 - The Philippines; Ven arrives in my life, in an envelope

My life changed completely when a couple of handwritten envelopes addressed in my name arrived at the main branch address at work. I was surprised because I did not have any communication with anyone anymore. When I opened them, they contained letters from America, Germany and China with photographs inside them. They were all about pen pals and I wondered how these guys had found my name and work address.

A few days later, my friend Belinda came into the shop and told me her pen pal from America was coming to see her. She explained that she had taken my photo and published my name in *International Correspondence* using my work address. She said she wanted to help me to find a good man and I should expect to receive many more pen pal letters from abroad soon! I didn't know what to say to her. I was scared, but happy that I would receive letters from different places abroad. She was completely right, and I received 21 letters. I was confused and did not know what to do with them, I didn't have good English and I was worried about how I could understand them, how I was going to write back and if I would understand their replies. One of the letters was a big brown envelope and when I opened it, there was a recorded cassette and three photographs inside. He was the only black person among all the people who wrote to me. I was scared and I did not read his letter straight away, because I had issues about black people. All I had heard about them before was bad. However, when I read his letter and listened to his voice recorded on the cassette, I was amazed!

On the tape, he introduced himself, told me about his background and he sang. The song was called, *Little Princess*, and it really hit me, and his wonderful voice captured my heart! His name was Venroy Wilks. Even typing his name right now brings back those memories and bring tears to my eyes. Little did I know that this first letter from Ven was the beginning of a long life journey!

I told Belinda about him and she was very pleased and encouraged me to get to know him. In fact, Ven and I became very close in a very short period of time through our correspondence. He sent me a recorded tape once a week, and in these he explained that he was originally from Jamaica in the West Indies and had gone to England to join his parents when he was 12 years old. I had never heard of Jamaica, but was delighted when Ven told me about it and sent me copies of his favourite reggae music. He liked all sorts of music, including classical, country western, and, of course, reggae. He introduced me to his favourite reggae artists by telling me about them and he recorded their songs for me, which eventually I got addicted to! He sent me a Sony Walkman and I went everywhere with it, listening to the songs he sent me.

Ven told me he started to work for the British railway and later became a train driver. He worked hard, did not drink much alcohol, and never smoked cigarettes. He loved to play tennis and football. We became very good friends and he encouraged and taught me so much. He told me to have a dictionary and read good books. I always looked forward to receiving his recorded tapes, which talked about many different things and contained many songs. He encouraged me to speak on the tape and practice my English and to ask him about anything I wanted to know. Although I was earning money from my job, Ven started to send me money regularly, even though I didn't ask for it. Slowly, I told him about my life and he felt compassionate towards me. In time, he said he was happy to have me as his girlfriend and he started to ring me at work once a week. He wanted to teach me to speak English and to practice it by talking with him. Sometimes he wanted to listen to me talk at the other end.

Chapter 2 - The Philippines; Ven arrives in my life, in an envelope

One Saturday morning, a customer asked me to take out the most expensive camera we sold and to demonstrate to him how to use it. While attending to him, a different customer asked me questions about another camera and, hoping for a sale, I attended to both of them at once. Little did I know, the two costumers were together! While I was answering the second customer's questions, the first customer ran away with the expensive camera and it took me few minutes to notice! Of course, I called the security guard, but he was a little slow and did not catch him. I knew at once that I was in a big trouble!

On the Monday morning, when I went to work, I was asked to report to my manager's office. He told me I had made a stupid mistake by taking the expensive camera out of the shelf and I had to cover the cost of it. I knew how much the camera was worth and it would take me a long time to pay for it. He asked me to sign an agreement for a certain amount to be deducted from my monthly wage until I finished paying the full amount of the camera. I was crying in front of him and was very distressed. When Ven rang me that week, I told him what had happened, but he told me not to worry because he would help me to pay it back. However, I was worried about it, because every time I received my wages, I didn't have much money left anymore to save.

At this time, my brother Jorge became ill and could not work, and Joel was unable to find a job. I barely had enough money to pay the rent and we struggled to buy food. Sometimes we had to either pay the rent or buy food; we could not do both. When we were a few months behind with our rent, the landlord asked us to move out. At the same time, Ven sent me a recorded tape explaining that he had financial problems and everything seemed against me. I was very down and discouraged. I continued to work but I was very miserable.

My only comfort was to read the beautiful poem, *Footprints in the Sand**. These words encouraged me and helped me cope with life.

Footprints in the Sand

*One night I dreamed a dream.
As I was walking along the beach with my Lord.
Across the dark sky flashed scenes from my life.
For each scene, I noticed two sets of footprints in the sand,
One belonging to me and one to my Lord.*

*After the last scene of my life flashed before me,
I looked back at the footprints in the sand.
I noticed that at many times along the path of my life,
especially at the very lowest and saddest times,
there was only one set of footprints.
This really troubled me, so I asked the Lord about it.
"Lord, you said once I decided to follow you,
you'd walk with me all the way.
But I noticed that during the saddest and most troublesome times of my life,
There was only one set of footprints.
I don't understand why, when I needed you the most,
You would leave me."*

*He whispered, "My precious child, I love you and will never leave you
never, ever, during your trials and testings.
When you saw only one set of footprints,
it was then that I carried you."*

Another lifeblood for me at this low point in my life was a gospel song by a local singer and actor in the Philippines called Gary Valenciano. I cried every time I listened to his popular song, *Lift Up Your Hands**. I did not know this song was taken from the Bible (Matthew 11:28-30). It comforted me, and Gary became one of my favourite actors and singers.

Chapter 2 - The Philippines; Ven arrives in my life, in an envelope

Lift Up Your Hands

*"Life is not at all but bad my friend, hmm… hmm …
If you believe in yourself
If you believe there's someone who walks through life with you
You'll never be alone, just learn to reach out and open your heart
Lift up your hands to God
And He'll show you the way."*

Uncle Democrito with my father Luis, 2007

You raise me up by Leila Wilks

The photograph of me, which my friend Belinda stole from me to publish in *International Correspondence*.

Ven and I the first day we met in the Philippines, 1993

Chapter 3 - Cebu and Cagayan: marriage and motherhood

Where we lived in Mabolo Mandaue Cebu, it was a squatter area with no vehicle access. There was parking outside the main road and it was a major fire risk area. Most people who lived there rented one room, like us, because the landlords simply extended their houses and rented it to workers and students. The rent was cheaper than anywhere else in the area. Our place was one big room. We had a table at the side with a sink beside it, together with a toilet and a place for washing clothes and to have a shower. We placed a small bed for me to sleep in around the corner of the room, with a curtain between the table and the bed. There were five of us who lived there, my four brothers and me. My brothers slept on the floor.

To walk from outside the main road to this place took five minutes, and went through a tiny public footpath between the walls of the other houses. One midnight, we were woken up by the noise of people screaming and shouting, 'Fire, fire, run!'

I woke up, but panicked and could not think what to do. Everyone was rushing to gather their possessions and running to the main road. My brother Abel told me to quickly get out and wait for him at the main road. He gathered our few possessions; I cried and was very scared and nervous. I rushed outside to the main road and called for my brother, Joe Marie. He had gone to help his girlfriend take out their possessions, instead of helping Abel to take out ours. However, Abel managed to take some of our possessions to the main road and I simply stood there watching and crying. It was a very shocking experience for us all that night. The whole place was burnt and we lost so many of our things, including many of Ven's letters and photographs. Fortunately, my brother Abel managed to take all the cassette tapes and the Walkman Ven had sent to me.

You raise me up by Leila Wilks

Early the next morning, we took a taxi to a relative, who was married and lived with her husband and daughter. We told her what had happened and asked her if we could stay with them until we found a new place to live. I was very disappointed to hear her say that she believed that if someone came to you from a fire disaster, you should not allow them to come into your house because it brings bad luck. She said she was very sorry, but she could not accept us into her home. I was annoyed because I had helped her in the past. She had lived with me for months when she had no money and I had helped her find a job. However, we did not have any choice and we decided instead to go to my friend Elisa, in Lahug Cebu. Without any question, she took us in and I went to work the next day hoping Ven would call and I could tell him what happened.

A few days later, he did call and I cried on the telephone with him. He promised to come and see me as soon as he had enough money. Shortly after, he sent me another recorded tape giving me many encouraging words and he sent me more money. He said he was there for me. He gave me several memorable sayings, which helped me at this point in my life.

- Over the clouds, there is a silver lining.
- There is always light at the end of the tunnel.
- Good things come to those who wait.
- I was his little princess.

Ven gave me hope in my life struggles.

We were struggling financially; Jorge still did not have work due to illness, and Joel could not find a job. What kept me going was Ven's recorded cassettes, his words of encouragement, his reggae music, and the various songs I listened to every day and at night on my Walkman. Because of the stress, I suffered a terrible asthma attack and my brother Jorge took me to a well-known

Chapter 3 - Cebu and Cagayan: marriage and motherhood

alternative doctor; not a medical doctor, because we didn't have the money for the hospital. I was given boiled roots from various plants and I stayed in this man's house with Jorge. I was there for a couple of weeks and slowly recovered. It was early in 1993 and, during this time, Ven sent me a recorded tape saying that he was coming to the Philippines to see me in March. I was very excited to hear this. He explained how concerned he was about me, because he had rung my work a few times, but never had any response.

The night before Ven was due to arrive at Mactan Airport, Cebu, I had a dream. I was lying in my bed and my mother was sitting on the edge. She said to me, "Ven is coming to see you. He is a good man and you need to look after him."

At five o'clock the next morning, Abel and I went to the airport to meet him. He was the first person off the plane, smiling from ear to ear! It was the most exciting thing that happened to me. I was the happiest person on earth that day. I ran towards him, and he was running towards me, and he lifted me up in his arms.

Abel helped him with his luggage and we went straight to the hotel we had booked for him. That day when he arrived, I completely forgot about my struggles. Ven and I went to the church and to the park, where we talked and talked about everything. We were so happy to have met at last and to discover that we were exactly who we said we were on the tapes to each other. It seemed as if we had known each other for years. He talked and talked, and I was so happy to listen. He told me how he had missed his connecting flight to Cebu and someone he met on the plane invited him to a club that night. The guy was Filipino and told him there was a lady singing there, who had a great voice. She sang a Whitney Houston song, *I will always love you*.

However, the lady really wanted to be with him. She held his hand while she sang, and afterwards she joined them on their table and sat on his lap.

But Ven told her, "My lady is waiting for me in Cebu," and he went back to the airport and waited for the next flight.

That same day, we went to see my cousin's husband Mike at his workplace at Sunburst Fried Chicken. Mike was very happy to meet Ven and we took a special photograph outside the restaurant; the first picture of Ven and I together.

With my brothers, we went home together to Alicomohan and stayed one night in Cagayan where we took Ven around the city. Ven was very happy to have roasted chicken in the middle of Cogon Market. He asked Nellie and Melchor, Nellie's husband, to come and stay one night with us in the hotel, and we talked and talked and had drinks together. Everyone in the family was very happy for me. We went to Alicomohan and stayed there in our house made of bamboo tree.

Ven has told me more about how hard life was growing up in Jamaica. His parents had left him with his aunt until he joined his parents in England when he was 12 years old. They also lived a hard life like me. I took Ven to Papa's farm and he enjoyed it there. He said it reminded him of his life in Jamaica.

A few days after his arrival in the Philippines, Ven asked me to marry him. I was very happy. He said he didn't want to go back to England a single man. He wanted to spend the rest of his life with me and we needed to be married. He could only stay for three weeks and suddenly we had a lot to do. Ven and I went to see various people to find out how we could be married in such a short period of time. Uncle Isabelo was very close to the Mayor in our town, Sugbongcogon, and he helped us to be married with a small family affair because we simply wanted it to be legal and to have the papers to back it up.

The day came when Ven had to return to England. That was very hard for me to cope with. We went to Cagayan de Oro City

Chapter 3 - Cebu and Cagayan: marriage and motherhood

Lumbia Airport to see Ven off. We were both crying; he reassured me he would be coming back to take me to his home in London.

I went through another tough experience after Ven left, and I didn't handle it well. I was suffering and feeling insecure and the same feeling of acute pain when I lost my mother came back.

I lost the desire to go back to Cebu to my job. I managed to get a place where Ven could ring me on a regular basis in Cagayan. I told him I had lost interest in going back to Cebu and he supportively said, "Leave the job and find another one in Cagayan, and you will be near your sister Nellie."

He said he would send me enough money to pay off the remaining amount for the camera I had lost. I followed Ven's suggestion and paid off the money before going back to Cagayan to stay with Nellie and Melchor. Ven was sending me money on a regular basis and I continued to look for a job. As usual, he was sending me recorded tapes expressing how he wanted me to join him as soon as possible.

More than a month after Ven left, while I was looking for a job, I suddenly felt very weak and ill, and I started to feel sick every morning. Later on, I found out I was pregnant. The thought of becoming a mother to my child was wonderful! I sat down and recorded a tape for Ven telling him the exciting news.

Nellie was pregnant at the same time and we watched Jacky Chan and Jean-Claude Van Damme action films. However, my pregnancy was tough and I craved rice with beef or rice with chicken, and I drank too much Coca Cola. I had terrible asthma attacks and it was hard to cope because I had limited medicines that I could take. I went to Alicomohan to join my father. He looked after me really well and bought home fresh fruit, vegetables and fish every day. I liked it there because there was fresh air and I enjoyed that time with my father. I was there for a couple of

39

months until I went back to stay with Nellie before I found a small place to rent. We went to the sea every morning as our mother had done and we stayed in the water together, keeping cool. Ven had booked a flight to come back to the Philippines when our baby was due, but he was delayed and arrived two days after our son, Jacky Jean, was born. We called him JJ.

Prior to the delivery, I was having contractions for more than a day, and I started to feel very weak. They moved me to another hospital to have a caesarean birth because the baby and I could have died. The day they operated on me, I only had a local anaesthetic, but when I looked to the left, on the wall I saw a framed picture of Jesus. I started praying in my mind, and in a few minutes I heard my baby cry! I was very happy. However, the next day I woke up with a terrible pain because the anaesthetic effect had worn off and I felt as if my belly was cut in half. I could not breastfeed JJ because of the excruciating pain. My family looked after my baby for me because I could not do anything but cope with the pain. My half-sister Enesia came to help me with JJ because she had worked in the hospital and knew what to do. When the nurse asked what the baby's name was I said Jacky Jean. I made this name up from Jacky Chan and Jean Claude Van Damme!

The third day after JJ was born, Ven arrived and my family and I met him at Lumbia City Airport in Cagayan. Melchor was holding his son Rhyme and my sister Enesia was holding JJ in her arms. Melchor tried to trick Ven and said to him, "This is your son."

Rhyme looked like a foreign child as well, but Melchor could not fool Ven. He walked across to my sister Enesia and said, "Boy, oh, boy" and shook his head. "This is my son!" He kissed JJ and everyone laughed.

Chapter 3 - Cebu and Cagayan: marriage and motherhood

Ven and I with uncles and aunties on our wedding day, 1993

You raise me up by Leila Wilks

Chapter 4 - Cebu to London; life, death, family and personal challenges

I was still in pain but I was thrilled to see my husband again, although Ven was only allowed to stay for three weeks in the Philippines. While he was there, we started the process of applying for my visa to go to the UK, together with JJ. We discovered that to marry me, Ven as a divorced person should have brought a letter of no impediment to prove he was free to marry me, according to our law. We also learnt he had to obtain this letter from the UK, accompanied by a letter of reference from his boss with his employment and income record.

Ven had less than three weeks to have this paperwork completed, and the Mayor's secretary did everything to the best of her ability to process the papers we needed. Little did we know that later in our lives we would face the consequences of rushing this through! It was a stressful time and we had a new baby to look after too.

On May 1st 1994, it was our annual fiesta celebration in Alicomohan, and my family all gathered there. Ven and I were processing paperwork and planned to join them the next day. But that evening, JJ suddenly became very sick. I was panicking because we did not have anyone to help us and I was still suffering the terrible pains from my caesarean operation. We were very worried watching our son vomiting, and I cried as I was watching him changing colour. He turned very dark and went very cold. We took JJ to the local hospital in a taxi, but we did not have any means of communication with my family in Alicomohan, and Ven and I were on our own to cope with the situation.

In the hospital, the nurses were not concerned about our son. They chatted to each other and one was applying her make-up. I was very annoyed and Ven was really angry to see that kind of poor service in a hospital. Back then, not a lot of Filipinos were married to foreigners and, seeing Ven, they were not interested to help us. We had to be very firm, but because I was not a firm person, Ven had to deal with them. Eventually they told us we had to wait until the doctor was available, but Ven insisted we had our son checked and that we couldn't wait for the doctor. I was very angry because I did not know how to deal with my own people. It is a sad situation when people can judge someone by the look of the person, not by checking out their character.

That was our first experience and test of life as a new family. Little did we know that later on, we would suffer many more struggles as a family with no one around to help. Poor little JJ was crying most of the time, but fortunately his health did improve after a week. After we all recovered from JJ's hospitalisation, we continued to assemble all the documents we needed for our visas to go to England. We went back and forth to many different offices, and there were many heated arguments between Ven and the authorities because they suddenly declared our marriage void.

This was a huge shock for both of us. The authorities told us that we had to marry again with the correct documents Ven needed from England. Ven was very stressed because he only had three days left to stay in the country. We went to the British Embassy in Manila and pleaded for their help; they were so kind to us. They said Ven could take us home to England, but we would need to marry again when we arrived to legalise the marriage. We were very happy to hear this and we were given the documents to back up their advice. However, when we went to the Philippine Embassy to give them these documents, they said I could go with Ven, but not JJ!

Ven was very annoyed and shouted, and had a heated argument with the Embassy staff. He said, "We are not leaving this office until you sign the papers that state the three of us can leave the

Chapter 4 - Cebu to London; life, death, family and personal challenges

country. I am not going back to England without my family." I was very unhappy hearing these unpleasant arguments between my husband and the Embassy staff. I was listening and feeling ignorant and useless. I was a very scared person when it came to people in authority, because I looked up to them. I had so much respect for them until that experience. We sat in their office for almost the whole day waiting. Ven rang the British Embassy and told them about the refusal for us to leave the Philippines. As I sat there, I remembered again what Granny Anastacia said to me: "Whenever you are in difficulty, ask God for help." I went to the corner so no one would notice me, and I whispered a prayer.

Seeing and hearing my husband fight with the authorities, and doing everything using his own knowledge and strength, I felt very emotional and wanted to do something to help him. The staff that Ven were dealing with ignored us. When they were getting ready to finish the day and were about to close their office, I suddenly heard my name being called. We rushed to the counter and were told they had received a note from the highest authority to say we could take our son with us to England, as long as Ven signed a document to say we will remarry as soon as we arrived. It was the same statement the British Embassy had given us. We cried together with relief and joy and we hugged little JJ. It showed us how British people care about children more than in my country, and I learnt a significant understanding from this experience. I also believed my prayers were answered, and I was very grateful in my heart.

Very quickly, the day came for us to leave the Philippines.

For me to leave my extended and close family was very hard. Although I went to various places far from my city on boats and long bus journeys, this one was much, much more scary, and it was my first time flying on a plane. In fact, I was terrified. Ven reassured me this feeling was normal for a person who had never travelled by plane before. He told me not to worry because I was with him.

We were to travel by boat from Cagayan to Manila, then by plane from Manila to Heathrow Airport in London, because we were running out of money and it was the cheapest way. However, the evening of our departure when we were ready to go to the port, a storm hit us without any warning. All day, we had sunshine with no storms forecast! My family were very sad to lose me and were coming to the port to see us off. However, in the sudden storm, we struggled to walk to the main road and soon we were soaking wet. My sister Nellie was holding JJ and made sure he was covered and did not get wet. I felt there was a strong force trying to stop us from leaving. We had to rush when we arrived at the boat and we nearly missed it!

All my family cried. They said to Ven, "Please look after our sister and JJ."

My brother Jorge took hold of Ven, looked him in the eye, and said, "Ven, look after yourself, so you can look after your family." Ven, impressed by that, was encouraged. Since Ven and I met, he and Jorge had got on very well. Jorge was the talker and joker in the family, and he had many talents. Ven admired and liked him because he made him laugh!

I was very scared when the plane was taking off. Ven held me tight and told me to close my eyes. I was so scared, I felt I was going to die. I cried but suddenly JJ started crying too and I had to attend to him. We went back and forth to the toilet because JJ was becoming very sick. He started to change colour again and became darker and his skin was very cold. I remembered we had some medicine left for him from the hospital and we gave this to him. It helped to calm him down and he slept in Ven's arms until we landed at Heathrow Airport.

I was very happy to arrive in England at last, but at the same time I was scared and worried because I did not have any family to call on to help me in my new life. Everything was different; I

Chapter 4 - Cebu to London; life, death, family and personal challenges

did not have good English to converse with people, and I was not a confident person. When we arrived in Woolwich, where Ven lived, I saw number 196 and knew it as our new home because I had written to Ven there so many times!

However, poor Ven didn't have any money left in his account even to buy a loaf of bread. He told me not to worry because he would be back at work in a few days and would be earning money again. He had simply been focusing on bringing his family to England and all we had to eat in the house was a tin of baked beans. Ven asked me to help him to search everywhere in the house to see if we could find £1 to buy a loaf of bread, and we did find the money under the bed!

Ven told me everything would change when he got back to work. He was very happy to have his family with him in England. Ven took me and JJ around the area and introduced us to his friends and his ex-wife Melva and his first son Otis, who was only eight years old.

When Ven went back to work, I was left in our flat alone with JJ. It was hard to cope with when I normally had a big family around me, and I felt lonely and scared about what sort of life was ahead of us. All I did was cry because Ven worked overtime to catch up with the bill payments, which had money owing. I was missing my family back home and I did not have anyone to talk to. One day, when Ven came home from work, he found me crying. He got JJ a pushchair to enable me to take him out. However, I was reluctant to go out because I was scared of meeting people who might talk to me. I was afraid I would not understand them and they would say I was stupid.

I became very negative and Ven suggested I phoned my family. This made me much happier but we ended up having a huge phone bill at the end of the month. One day, Ven took me and JJ to his work and introduced us to his friends and colleagues.

His manager said to me, "You are a very special woman because Ven went through a lot to get you and your son over here." Ven took us into the cab on the train he was driving and we were so happy. The scenery was beautiful and that experience gave me the courage to go out with JJ.

Months passed, and I received a sad phone call from my family. Nellie and Melchor's second son Mark had died. He was only eight years old. I was devastated because I was very close to him when I was there and I cried like a baby, even though Ven did his best to comfort me, but he was shocked too. I felt useless because we were not in a position to go home to attend his funeral. I was very sad and it took me a while to recover.

A few months later, Granny Anastacia died. I was close to her too and she was the one who had protected me from my father when he was beating me up as a child. She always supported and encouraged me every time I visited her. She told me, "In the middle of trials and sufferings, whenever you feel lost and empty, always remember the Lord is there to help you. Call on him."

I wanted desperately to go home and see her for the last time but we did not have the money. I was far away from home and I felt helpless; I could not do anything but cry.

Ven introduced me to his brothers, his sister Sarah, and his sister-in-law, Yvonne and her children, Aaron and Rosie. Yvonne and I became good friends from the day we met.

I must have been a very miserable person to live with that first year of our marriage because of the grief I was suffering and a longing to see my family. Sometimes I did not talk to Ven for days and he ended up talking to JJ, even though he couldn't understand him. I started looking for ways to irritate him so he would send me home!

Chapter 4 - Cebu to London; life, death, family and personal challenges

I was getting worse and worse, and I remember when I went to the children's clinic. I talked to the staff nurse and told her, "I do not want to be with my husband any more," and asked what did she think I could do. She looked at me sternly and said, "You want me to deal with your problem that is not my job. It is your problem and you must deal with it!"

I cried all the way home and was confused about what was wrong with me. It was strange after all the hard work Ven had done to bring us to England that I didn't remember or appreciate it. I didn't have anyone to talk to. I avoided having long conversations on the phone with my family because we would have a huge phone bill to pay, and it did not make sense to me to make my family feel worried about me. I kept everything inside but I took it all out on Ven, which was very unpleasant. However, he gently helped me by making many good suggestions.

He said, "Listen to *talkRADIO* and it will help you understand people and the way they speak. You will learn from them."

I started to do this, but I was still depressed and homesick.

One time when I was very angry and confused, I started crying and begging Ven to send me back to my country. He was angry! I suppose he'd had enough of my bad behaviour.

He shouted and said, "You are going crazy! Have you forgotten how hard it is to live in your country and how your own people give you a hard time? They do not really care about you!"

I was angry because this was the truth, and when we hear the truth, it hurts! Because I was angry, I went straight to the door and I wanted to leave.

Ven said, "Where are you going?"

"Anywhere. No one cares!" I replied.

JJ started to cry, and Ven said, "You need to attend to your son."

But I said, "You do it, I am going!"

JJ was crying hard so he went to attend to him and I went out of the front door. He started calling me and holding JJ in his arms. He ran after me. But I ran fast straight towards Woolwich Arsenal Station and he did not see me. I got on the train to London Bridge Station and it was late, around 9pm. I sat there and cried like a baby. I was there for an hour and it got quieter and I felt scared. I got on the train and went back to our flat.

Ven was very angry with me, but he was honest, and said, "I do not want you to do that again. You are a grown woman and you have a family here. Do not focus only on yourself because I have to work and you are giving me a hard time. If you do not stop, you might regret what will happened in the future."

I did not talk to him but everything he said registered in my head. I understood it. My feelings were up and down and I knew I had to change my attitude. My mind was willing to do what was necessary to change, but the actual actions I took were the opposite. I did not understand myself. I blamed myself for being selfish and not thinking about my immediate family.

Chapter 4 - Cebu to London; life, death, family and personal challenges

Ven and I in our flat in Woolwich, London

You raise me up by Leila Wilks

Chapter 5 - London; the rat race, from cleaner to business owner

The following year, I received my permanent residence permit in England and Ven found me a cleaning job. It was for the same company he worked for but in a different place, and I started working at the train depot in August 1995. Ven was on night shifts and I was working in the day. I took JJ with me on my way to work and I met Ven at London Bridge, who took JJ home with him. When I came home in the evening, Ven was getting ready for work! It was good family planning, we thought, and we wouldn't have any more children, but actually this was not good for our relationship.

I was determined to help Ven pay our mortgage and the bills every month. We continued this life for a couple of years, until one day when I had changed to the night shift and Ven was working days. I was home with JJ and fell asleep in our bedroom. Our flat was on the third floor facing the road below, and because I was very tired, I forgot to close the window. While I was asleep, JJ climbed up to the window from our bed and, with half his body over the windowsill, was waving to the people walking on the pavement! Luckily, I woke up and saw when JJ was trying to climb out of the window! I was terrified!

This episode changed everything and we had to find a childminder. It stretched us financially and it was a hard thing for me to cope with knowing someone else was looking after my son while I was at home in the day sleeping so I could go back to work during the night.

I had sleepless days in the first few months and so did Ven, but we didn't have a choice. The company offered me overtime and sometimes I worked at the weekends as well. There were months when I was working seven days a week. Ven was home at the weekends and we didn't realise how we had been caught up in the 'rat race'.

Many people we knew were in a similar position, with no time for the family. However, I started to save money, thinking we could buy a piece of land back home to build a house when we go home to visit the family. We were struggling financially, but I was doing my best to save a small amount every month. Ven also had to find weekly financial support for his first son Otis, and one week we did not have enough money to buy fresh food.

I continued to work seven days a week, but the more money I earned, the more tax I paid! During this time in London, I felt there was something missing in my life. Since I started to work at the weekends, I had stopped going to church and stopped praying. No matter how hard Ven and I worked, we never had enough money. We were always behind with our bills.

One evening, on the way home from work, Ven met a Jamaican man who told Ven about a business where you could leave your job and become financially free. He said he knew a couple called Roger and Paula Galloway, who were building this multi-level marketing business and who had retired at 29 years old. When they came round to our house to talk with us about it, Ven became very excited. He asked me to support him to try out this new business idea, which although I did not feel sure about, I agreed.

During this time, JJ had regular asthma attacks and we took him to the hospital every week. They were very difficult moments for any parent to see. He looked at us, struggling for breath and said, "Mum, Dad, I can't breathe, I'm scared."

I cried every time he was in the hospital, holding his hand and talking to him. I remember Ven saying to JJ, "I wish I could breathe for you, my son," and walking away crying.

Chapter 5 - London; the rat race, from cleaner to business owner

Whenever I was on day shift, Ven and I went out in the evening to build the business. I started to understand the benefit it offered us if we worked at it. I was still not confident, but I liked it because I was spending more time with my husband and we were working together for our future. We started close to home and slowly broadened our horizons, expanding the business into different areas nearby, and we attended our first business seminar where we met Roger and Paula. They had great energy and enthusiasm, and everyone loved them. They had successfully built an international business and were financially free. Roger had retired from his full-time job at 29 when their first son, Jamie, was only a couple of months old. Their children never saw them going out to work. They were a hard-working and very dedicated couple. Little did I know that later they would become good friends, real family to us, as well as business mentors, and they would do more than we could ever imagine for us.

Ven had seen how dedicated Roger was about building the business, and he was willing to help us if we had the same approach. At the business seminar, I was nervous about meeting new people, but I was willing to listen to the speakers and learn what I could. When they started recognising people for reaching different levels in the business, I began to understand the opportunities ahead of us. We had hope for the future now, working with Roger and Paula's team. It was amazing; they were honest, enthusiastic people, and they had a genuine interest in our success as well.

Due to my frequent sickness from work, my manger eventually got the message and allowed me to work day shifts at last! I was very happy because it meant Ven and I were able to build our business. I was available most evenings and my health improved because I was sleeping at night again.

One weekend, Ven and I were invited by Roger and Paula to go to a Health Training Seminar. We were in their car travelling for a couple of hours, and I remember feeling very uncomfortable. I looked up to them highly and always put myself down. I thought, compared with them, I was nothing. But they always helped me to feel comfortable by talking to me, asking me about my family and JJ. In the first couple of years of working in the business, I slowly gained confidence in meeting people. It helped that I was in a very warm and friendly environment where no one criticised me. We went to a business seminar once a month and to a business conference three times a year. Ven was very determined to work in the business, but I was the one who kept the records of our clients, and did the follow-up and made appointments on the phone. At first, I was not comfortable making the phone calls, but the thought that we were working together for our future gave me courage.

Ven delivered the presentations, sharing the business with people, and being an outgoing person who loved to chat to people he did well, and this encouraged me. I asked Ven not to embarrass me in front of people and not to force me to talk to them, and I promised to work in the business in my own style. He said, "No problem!"

He could see my willingness, despite not feeling comfortable with people. I also asked him not to introduce me as his wife when we met people on the train travelling to meetings. I used to sit in the corner and leave Ven chatting with people!

I was very fortunate because in the business, our team leaders had a *Book of the Month* programme. They selected books for us to read to develop our confidence and have more understanding about people's behaviour and about running a small business. We also had a *Tape of the Month* programme with different speakers who were well known in the business arena. I remember I refused to have the books, because I did not like reading, but I really enjoyed listening to the tapes because I was able to listen to them on my Walkman when I travelled to work. I remember how, before I had a job or started with the business, Ven encouraged

Chapter 5 - London; the rat race, from cleaner to business owner

me to read books. Sadly, I didn't listen to him, although he left books around the house for me to pick up. Ven, like me, always enjoyed listening to music tapes. He had his own Walkman for when he travelled to work as well. We went to talk to our business mentor and asked him to stop ordering these monthly books for us. He explained that we might not see the result straight away from what we learnt from reading these books, but he promised they would help us to develop our confidence and our characters. He told us they would also help us with our marriage and how to deal with people we met every day and he encouraged us to read the books. Eventually, I started to read the books and, to my surprise, they were brilliant!

Once when we were going to our monthly seminar, I noticed one of Ven's books lying about at home and I showed it to him. He said he had read the book a long time ago and it was great, that's why he had wanted me to read it. Ven had a few good books at home he had bought for himself, and I believe they helped him to develop and grow. Our leaders in the business encouraged us to read for 20 minutes a day, and I slowly got into this habit. For the first few months, I fell asleep every time I started to read. But when the books started making a big difference to my confidence, I understood that knowledge is powerful and encouragement is vital in any difficult situation.

When I look back, it was the way Ven and our business mentor encouraged me that made all the difference. I worked hard in my job and the business, and gradually we developed many friendships. Ven and I were encouraged whenever we met an ordinary person like us who had been successful in using the business as their vehicle to financial freedom. We thought, "If they can do it, so can we!"

I also found the letters my family wrote to me very touching, especially my father's letters. They helped to inspire and motivate me to make my life in London a success.

You raise me up by Leila Wilks

> Dec. 28 - 2000
>
> Menakal cong mga anack
> Leila, Venroy & Jacky Jean.
> (nadawat co ang imong manga letrato ug sangco sa langit acong calipay que haloc halocan co tongod sa daco cong calipay nga dugay na wala na kita mag ca uban, labina gayod sa bata, panga mosta lang co ni Venroy gg. ug fina ut unta nga tag-a-an camo pirme sa ma-ayong pang lawas, camong tanan ma-oy acong calipay sa acong kinabuhe, malipayon aco con makita co ang mga letrato.) atua caron nilang Nellie ug Geniliza ug.
>
> Imong Amahan
>
> Capus
>
> Linoy Pas

"I have received your photos and my happiness has reached the sky! I kissed it lots of times for so much joy. It's been a long time that we are not together, especially the baby (JJ). Say hi to Venroy and JJ. And I hope you are always in good health. You all have given me happiness in my life, I am so happy whenever I see your photos."

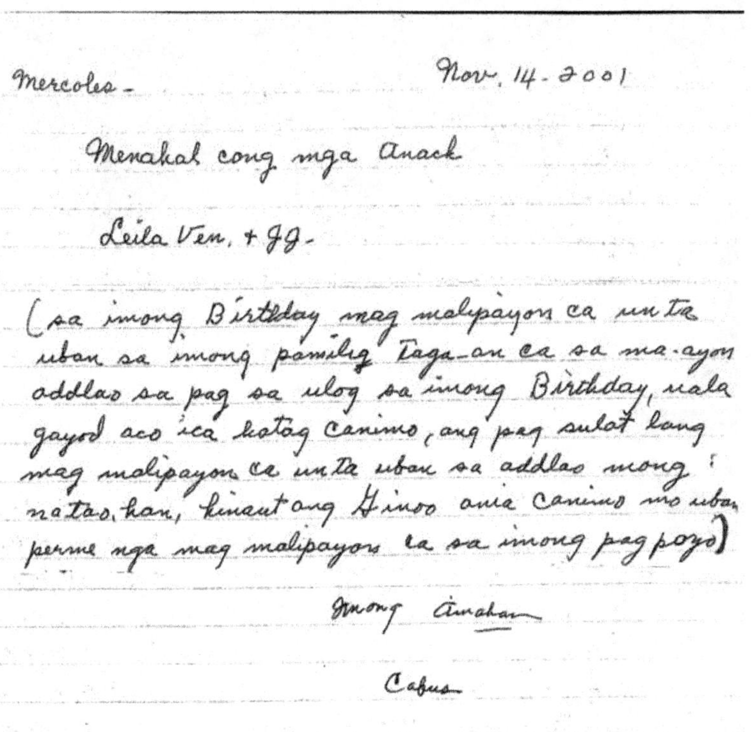

Mercoles - Nov. 14-2001

Menahal cong mga Anack

Leila Ven, + JJ-

(sa imong Birthday mag malipayon ca unta uban sa imong pamilig Taga-an ca sa ma-ayon addlao sa pag sa ulog sa imong Birthday, uala gayod aco ica hatag canimo, ang pag sulat lang mag malipayon ca unta uban sa addlao mong natao,han, kinaut ang Ginoo auia canimo mo uban perme nga mag malipayon ca sa imong pag pozo)

Imong Amahan

Cabua

"On your birthday, may you be happy with your family and you will have a nice day to celebrate it. I do not have anything to give you but this letter to wish you a happy birthday. I hope the Lord will always be with you and you are always happy in your life.
Your poor father
Luis Y. Pao"

You raise me up by Leila Wilks

Ven, Roger, Paula and myself having dinner together, 1996

Ven, myself, Glory, Tina, Nellie, Jenny, Joanna (our cousin), Joe Marie and his wife Yvonne during a business seminar

Chapter 6 - London; personal growth and a flourishing business

Ven continued to drive trains from King's Cross to Peterborough or to Cambridge, until British Rail was privatised and he started to experience tremendous pressure. He worked for very long hours without a rest because they were cutting costs and there were a lack of drivers. Ven complained when he came home about how tired and fed up he was with his job. He hated the situation he was in and it hurt him when he came home from the night shift and JJ was not there, because he was already at the childminder's. Sometimes he couldn't sleep during the day before his shift so he went to be with JJ. He wanted to leave his job to escape this situation.

Then he began to develop high blood pressure. The train drivers' income was good, but the pressure of work was unbearable because of the new management. They announced they would offer severance to those drivers who wanted to leave the company and Ven decided it was time to leave. He did not get a huge pay out but he was so happy to leave. We invested his severance money and he stayed at home to look after JJ.

Two years passed after Ven took severance, and he was at home spending time with JJ and taking him to school. I started to feel the pressure of having to work seven days a week again, but at least this time I was on permanent day shift. It is amazing how we thought we could do more in the business when he was at home. We did do a lot for a short time after he took the severance, but eventually when I needed to work longer hours, I could not be with him and we were not as active in the business during those years. I suppose this was our stage of growth, personally and mentally. We were reading during this time and listening to the tapes. We felt we were doing something in the business by studying.

At the weekend, Ven drove me to work and picked me up. He encouraged me to learn to drive so I could go anywhere I wanted when I was ready, but this was the last thing I wanted to do; I did not have any interest in learning to drive! I slept in our car while Ven was driving me to work and also on the way home. I had again stopped going to church again because I was working every weekend. Our life was very tough and I became a very miserable person to live with again! Reading books and listening to the inspirational tapes was really the only thing which helped us to carry on during that hard period. I had stopped praying to God because I was too tired most of the time. In the business, I started to work very closely with Paula and she showed me how to earn more money using the skin care and make-up products.

Roger and Paula helped us develop the business, and always encouraged us and praised us when we did small things in our business. I went to make-up training events and learnt a lot. Paula encouraged me to go to these events because there was money there. I was still nervous about meeting new people, but these events were helping me and I picked up the courage to do it. Ven said to me, "Don't be afraid because I will be there with you when you do the presentations. I will be at the back and I will talk to the women."

The first skin care and make-up event I delivered was to 13 women. Before leaving home, I rang Paula and she encouraged me. She said she was confident in me and I was going to be fine. Ven was the only man in the room. Fortunately, the women did not mind him being there! I was very nervous but I knew what I was doing because I had completed the training. This knowledge was really important because no matter how scared I was, I had all the notes with me and I simply read out the important things and conducted the demonstrations. It was very good to hear Ven in the background say, "That's my little lady!"

Chapter 6 - London; personal growth and a flourishing business

I was very proud of myself after I finished the presentation. We earned a lot of money that day in only one session. Going home, Ven gave me a big hug and said, "I am very proud of you. You really did that well."

Hearing that from my husband really helped my confidence! I talked to Paula about the success and we all felt very happy.

As a result of that success, I delivered more presentations, and the more presentations I did, the more confident I became. Ven was there with me most of the time because he had to drive me to the places and I had a lot of products to carry. Ven was my knight in shining armour. He was always there to support me, although sometimes it still annoyed me to see him always smiling and talking to people without any problem. He talked to people and always managed to look happy despite our financial difficulties. He always had something to talk about. I felt as if I was a very miserable person at home; I don't know how he put up with me.

My weakness was I didn't like to talk whenever I was tired, and I was always tired! In our flat, it must have seemed as if there was only Ven and JJ and my voice was hardly there. When Ven did something that upset me, I would not talk to him for weeks. I worried about many things in my heart while Ven enjoyed life. It made me angry that I had to take care of everything and work away from home while he enjoyed himself.

Eventually, I learnt that all my worrying was not accomplishing anything good. Instead it gave me headaches, made me more nervous and grouchy, and achieved nothing beneficial. Because of the way I was behaving, Ven started to talk to me very firmly, and at times he was really annoyed with me. I could see his patience was tested to the full. Once he said to me, "You are a very difficult person to understand. If you continue to behave like this, we might not last a very long time together."

He was very serious when he said this. I remember a few times before going to sleep at night, Ven would turn to me and say, "We should be talking to each other. You should stop behaving like that, not talking to me, because I have not done anything bad, as far as I'm concerned. We should not go to bed feeling angry towards each other, because one of us might die tomorrow and we wouldn't forgive ourselves.'"

Hearing that made me feel guilty and scared. I did not talk to him straight away because of pride, but I slowly moved closer to him without saying anything.

He hugged me and said, "I know you don't mean any harm. You are upset about something. Try to express yourself to me and I will try to understand you."

Every time I did not talk to him before he went to sleep at night, he said the same thing again. Slowly, I started to change the way I behaved and I learnt how to communicate with my husband and how to express myself to him. I started telling him about the things that upset me, and eventually he did less of the things that annoyed me. When I started to develop confidence within myself, I started to talk to Ven for hours before we went to bed. I talked about my experiences at work and at home. But when I found out sometimes he fell asleep while I was talking, I was annoyed with him again and stopped talking. I was upset and told him off in the morning!

He said to me, "Darling, please do not stop talking to me. What it is, the longer you talk, the more comfortable I feel. Your voice to me is like music in my ears."

Later in life, the same thing happened with our son, JJ. He liked to listen to me talking, but fell asleep like his dad! But it did not annoy me anymore. It made me laugh! However, Ven always showed his admiration towards me. Whenever we went out to business meetings, he would recommend clothes for me to wear and say to other people, "This is my little lady!"

These things really helped developed my self-image, plus I was reading books every day; in fact, I was reading more than he was at this time. I was now the one who reminded him to read. He then had a problem with his eye, enough of an excuse not to read. We went to the optician and came home with reading glasses for him, but when we went out on the train, he would forget to take his reading glasses, and I would take them for him whenever I remembered. Anyway, Ven would prefer to talk to people on the train rather than sit down in the corner with a book. Reading the books and listening to tapes daily really helped me to feel more confident. I was changing from the inside.

I was still nervous in the presence of Roger and Paula, and I told myself that I would never normally mix with rich people because I was poor and they would never want to become my friends. It took me a few years to be comfortable with successful people. We were meeting lots of people who were financially free by now. I was still quiet and used to beat myself up mentally, putting myself down all the time and placing successful people up on a pedestal. However, the business team encouraged me to continue to read and listen to inspirational tapes every day.

There had been a lady I worked with in my cleaning job who was very hard to get on with, and she never acknowledged my daily "Good Morning" greeting. She didn't even look at me, but I noticed she was the same with everyone. Later, I read a book about attitude and learnt it was about the other person, not me! When people are nasty and hard to deal with, keep your attitude up; it's them who have a problem. They are not happy about something in their life, and you don't have to be like them. I learnt to control my thoughts, to control my feelings. As the years went by, I started to change and found it easier to talk to anyone. I stopped looking down on myself, stopped criticising myself and started to be more positive. I practiced the Success Principle I had learnt from the books I read. At the same time, our business started to grow and I realised I had to grow inside first before our business could expand.

Although we had been working hard, we were not getting good results. I did not realise that success partly depended on our attitudes. I saw that whatever we put in our minds came out somehow, whether they were positive or negative thoughts. We started to see great results from our efforts and we were meeting many positive people. I had started to attract positive thinking people. I began to talk to more of the office staff at work and I became friendly with our company manager. He teased me when we travelled together on the train because he saw me with a book in my hand all the time. He became curious and started to read a few lines from my book and was impressed. He asked to borrow a few of my books. I read books written by Og Mandino, Norman Vincent Peale, Dale Carnegie, Napoleon Hill, Dr. Robert Schuller, John Maxwell, and many more.

Ven and I attended regular leadership seminars because, by this time, we were leading our own group of people. I now felt comfortable being with Roger and Paula, and we felt blessed to be a part of this business system. All the people who had been working with us, apart from Roger and Paula, had decided not to continue building the business. Roger and Paula became our close friends and we were working directly with them and were personally mentored by them. They would do anything to help us, not only with the business but with our personal situation as well. If one of us was sick, they were the first people to support us and offer help. I remember one situation when we had to redecorate our flat and we needed help. Ven's family couldn't help but Roger drove all the way from Middlesex to our area in south-east London to help us clear up our flat and throw the rubbish away. He drove there every day until we finished the work. He was a brother and a mentor to us! And Paula was too. Every

Chapter 6 - London; personal growth and a flourishing business

time I needed to talk to a sister, I phoned Paula and talked about everything with her. They helped us in many different ways. All the encouragement and support was there. They would never talk negatively about anything or anyone. Ven and I were very inspired by them. Even when I was a hard person to live with, they were always kind and understanding. They never talked down to us. They always tried to build us up.

I remember Roger saying, "You know, Ven really loves you," and to hear that was very reassuring, although I knew I did not deserve to be loved at that time. I did not do what a good and loving wife would do for her husband. All those things went out of the window because life was such a constant struggle.

Ven started to look for another job. He'd had enough of my behaviour and, practically, he needed to be occupied and to work. He applied for a driving job in the Thameslink train company, but they turned down his application because of his severance from King's Cross. Eventually, he found a job as a security officer in Dartford Job Centre. I asked him if he was sure about doing this job, but he said it didn't matter whatever it was, as long as he had a job. In fact, Ven was transferred to Woolwich Job Centre where we lived and this gave him more time to build our growing business. There were positive changes between Ven and I too. He was reading books again and I was hearing great feedback about Ven's performance at work. People came to him for encouragement, and he got on well with his work colleagues and most of their clients enjoyed his company. Ven had great people skills and he could turn a bad situation into a peaceful one.

Life improved for us financially and also with our marriage and our relationship. I was able to go back to normal working hours from Monday to Friday. We were able to live a more balanced life with work, family and the business. I went back to church again most Sundays.

However, in 2003, Ven started to feel sick and he had to stay at home a few times. I asked him to go and see the doctor but he'd say he was fine. However, once when I came home, he was lying down in the bedroom. He told me he felt dizzy and had vomited. He still went to work until the staff sent him home. I had to be firm with him and he promised me he would see the doctor this time. He recovered and because it did not happen again, he never did see the doctor.

Then one day when Ven was at work, he felt very weak and very sick, so he went to our local medical clinic. As soon as Dr. Coutinho saw him, she said, "Ven, you need to be admitted into hospital right now!"

Ven was very sick and was in hospital for a week. He had high blood pressure and kidney failure. Since our marriage, this was the first time I had seen Ven in a hospital. I was very worried about him. I was on my own and had no family around to help. I rang Roger and Paula and told them about it. At home that week with JJ, I felt scared and very worried. I cried talking to my JJ, holding his hand and saying, "I am worried about Daddy," and JJ looked at me smiling; it was as though he was trying to say Daddy would be fine.

Ven was a very emotional person. He cried that day and thanked me. He should have seen a doctor sooner, at those times when he was sick, but he had ignored it. Until then, Ven had been a very active person; he played tennis every weekend and loved it and it kept him fit. I informed some of Ven's family. We both learnt a lesson from this experience. Each body is unique; whenever something is wrong inside our system, we receive a signal, such as a headache, dizziness and more. We really should not ignore it. Every sign needs to be checked.

We had a product delivery the week Ven was in hospital and I did it on my own. I felt very lonely travelling and doing our business alone. I went to a business meeting Roger and Paula were hosting where they talked about commitment. I remember Paula said that all of us have challenges to face in life. We can stop doing what we are doing and let these challenges control us, or we can decide to be in control of them. They applauded me for being there, despite Ven being in hospital, but for me, it was not an option, I had to be there. Ven and I learned that to become successful in life, we have to be fully into what we are doing, and there is no half effort, we are either all in or all out, no in between, and we needed to have patience and determination. From a farming background, I fully understand this principle. In everything, there is a season.

On the farm, we prepared the soil, planted the seeds and watered them if there was no rain. The crop grew and we waited for the harvest. It is a process and a journey too. It was very fortunate that Ven and I came from a similar poor farming and family background. We went through the same struggles in life when we were young and we understood the cycle. Ven and his brothers had walked through the mountains in Jamaica to find food to eat. We knew that life struggles make us a better person, or a bitter person. It is our choice.

Ven's hospital experience had shaken me on the inside. It was a warning for us. I felt the taste of a very lonely life. I was used to spending my life with Ven and every evening we were together. A week without him in our home was an experience I was not prepared to go through again. I felt scared, sad, empty and very lonely. JJ and I were very glad when Ven came out of hospital after a week. It felt like months to me.

From then on, I had to monitor his intakes. He had to take eight tablets a day to control his blood pressure and blood flow. I bought him all the multivitamins he needed to take every day. He had to stay at home for nearly a month to rest and to continue the treatment. The doctor in King's College Hospital told him that he wouldn't be able to play tennis for years, but Ven didn't believe what the doctor said. He was positive he would be able to play tennis sooner than the doctor had predicted and, amazingly, six months after his hospitalisation, Ven was back to normal again and playing tennis! I could see he was as strong as he used to be as I watched him.

We continued to be successful in our business. We qualified for a few promotions the company offered and we regularly attended business leadership seminars. The positive changes in me showed in my performance at work. I was much happier. As we had learnt, positive people attract positives, and negative people attract negatives. I made a lot of friends at work and I had a good friendship with my supervisor. Everyone saw the changes in me. I became more active and involved at work, and took on additional responsibilities, which I enjoyed. It took me years to develop the confidence to approach someone and say, "Hi!" But I achieved it!

Chapter 7 - London, Jamaica, the Philippines; family travels

One day, my manager's son came to work with his wife from Thailand. She was a beautiful 26-year-old lady, very attractive and friendly. My manager and her son took her to the platform where we were working and showed her what we were doing. Three days after that, my manager's daughter-in-law started to work with us. She did not speak much English. I was glad to meet her and to know she would be working with us because she and I looked like sisters, though she was taller than me and younger. A few of the people at work even thought she was my sister. Her name was Anita and we became close friends. We sat at the same table and always had our lunch together. Anita and I talked about our families back home. As Asians, we are very family-oriented people. She told me about her experiences and her life struggles back home. We worked together on the trains and we talked non-stop about everything!

My manager never invited us to her birthday party, but Anita decided to invite us and we went. Anita was my number one business customer at work and she bought many products from our business, which supported my success in the health and make-up side. She also cooked delicious Thai food and sold meals at work. She quickly built up a following of regular customers, including me. Anita was a sensitive person and she loved people. She was a giver and she liked to help people, and found it very hard to live with people who weren't the same. Anita also liked to laugh and tell jokes. She once had three weeks off work and went home to Thailand with her husband to visit her family. When she came back, she brought me a nice blouse and skirt, a pair of sandals and a lovely necklace, which I still have today.

I remember when she gave me the necklace. She said to me, "You will always remember me when you see this necklace. I do not have a lot to give you but these gifts."

I said, "This is so much!" and thanked her sincerely.

However, when she came back from her holiday, I noticed several changes in her. She was very quiet and wanted to be on her own more. I asked her if something was wrong and could I do something to help. But she said, "Thank you, Leila, but there's nothing you can do to help me."

However, she started to act more and more strangely. As usual on a Friday, we wished each other a good weekend and a good rest. But one Friday, she added, "Thank you, Leila, for being so nice to me and such a good friend."

"Well, I like you. Don't worry about things, simply pray," I told her.

Previously, I had been talking to her about how important it is to believe in God, because He is there to help us in everything we are going through.

She smiled that day and said, "Goodbye, Leila."

On the Monday morning when I came to work, I heard that Anita had an epileptic attack on the Saturday and was in a coma in the hospital. I was shocked and I cried. We were all disturbed by the news. Most of us were very worried about her because all the staff in our department loved her. As I was doing my job that day, I cried and so did several of the other women. Anita had made a lot of friends at work, but I was the closest one to her. She talked to almost everyone and her English had really improved. My manager called a few of my work colleagues together and told them what had happened, and one of my work colleagues told me what she'd said to them. A week after that, my manager asked a few of my colleagues to visit Anita in the hospital. I asked the manager if I could go too, but she said she only wanted a few people to go. I was very disappointed because I was very desperate to see Anita. I wanted to talk to her and I was sure she would listen to me. I did not understand why her mother-in-law did not want me to visit her, when they all knew I was close to her.

I told Ven about it and how it hurt me and how I was struggling to deal with it. Ven encouraged me to be strong and to keep on talking to him about how I felt, knowing that Anita had become almost like a sister to me.

One night, I dreamt about Anita. She was smiling and we were talking, but suddenly she said to me, "I must go now, Leila and thank you." I saw her walking away, waving her hand, until I could not see her anymore, and she disappeared.

When I woke up, I started crying because I knew she had come to say goodbye to me in that dream, before she died in the hospital. On my way to work in the morning, I was very sad and tearful. I saw a work colleague on the train who asked me if I would go and visit Anita. I could not answer because I knew in my heart she was already dead. As soon as we arrived at work, our colleagues met us at the door and told us Anita had died in the night.

I was not surprised because I knew before they did. I did not say anything and went straight to our locker room and cried with my work colleagues. A few days after that, our manager announced that anyone who wanted to attend Anita's cremation were all welcome, but I said, "No, I want to keep her alive in my memory."

After Anita's death, I lost my desire to work there. I really felt very emotional about the whole incident. It was 2005 and Ven saw my struggle and understood how hurt I was. We decided we needed to go for a holiday, so we went to Jamaica for three weeks and had a great time. I met Ven's father, together with his second wife and Ven's eldest brother, for the first time. We stayed with Ven's father in Saint Catherine, Spanish Town, and his brother drove us everywhere. Ven took JJ and I to his school and showed us the tree where he used to sit with his friends. We also went to visit Ven's cousin, who Ven and his brothers used to live with while his parents were in England working to raise the money for them to follow.

One day, we went out with Ven's sister Sarah and her daughter, Antoinette. We went to Kentucky Fried Chicken to eat and to the park. Afterwards, we went to visit the place where Bob Marley used to live in Kingston! We took many photos and it was a very happy memory for us.

The following year, 2006, we decided to visit my family in the Philippines for the first time since coming to England, and I was very excited. I had already bought a piece of land in Cagayan and we started to build a three-bedroomed house, because Ven and I had been sending money home ahead of our visit. We arrived in Cebu City in April 2006, and my brother Abel and his wife Nila, with their son Abnil, met us at the airport. I was so happy to see my brother and his family again. We caught a boat from Cebu to our city in Cagayan. Ven was fascinated by the boat and was very excited walking up and down, meeting people and talking with them.

When we arrived at Cagayan de Oro City pier, we were met by the rest of my family, which was amazing! It was a very special time for us. My family had made a large sign saying, "Welcome home, Ven, Leila and JJ."

The next day, we attended my brother Joe Marie's wedding. I was not fully prepared and a little jet-lagged, but he had planned

Chapter 7 - London, Jamaica, the Philippines; family travels

his wedding to include us and I was very glad we attended. After the wedding, we spent time buying what we needed for the house project and we went to visit Papa and my many relatives in Alicomohan. The place had sentimental value to me, and Ven knew that. On our way back, we stopped at the beach and enjoyed the atmosphere.

A few days later, we met the international leader of our business, who was based in the Philippines. We had been introduced by telephone from England, but the leaders in the Philippines wanted to meet us and our business leader was there, who later became our mentor in the Philippines. Glory Tan owned a long-established business and she invited us to her business seminar. Ven and I had a great time meeting everyone and learning about how they were building up their business because we knew we could do it too with the contacts we had in the Philippines.

We held many business meetings, and in the four weeks we were there, we were able to draw a big team together. We wanted to develop a massive business there and Glory worked well with us to make it happen. We also travelled with our family and this made Ven happy because he started to feel at home with my family plus we had the opportunity to meet new people. The four weeks passed very quickly, and when it was time to return to the UK, my family came to the port to see us off. It was a very sad moment for us all to separate again.

When we were back in England, JJ started year eight at school. He was not very comfortable initially and experienced a few months of unpleasant bullying from the other children. However, when he was picked for a football team to compete in a local tournament, he started to settle in again. One evening, Ven and I had a long discussion about our future and we made a new life action plan because Ven had a vision of setting up a huge business in the Philippines. We were not in good circumstances in London. Ven had been taking eight tablets every day to control his blood pressure, JJ was not happy in school and I had lost interest in going to work since Anita had died. We discussed it for a week; we decided to sell our flat and go home to the Philippines for good. The more we talked about it, the more enthusiastic we became. We shared our plans with Roger and Paula and they were open-minded about it because they could see the positive side. Although it was a big decision, we were more focused on the end result. In addition, Ven was not happy at work and the stress was starting to build up in him again, which was something he needed to avoid because of his blood pressure problem. We discussed our decision with Roger, Paula and the rest of the leaders in our organisation, and they all gave us their blessings.

It was exciting. Ven and I started the process straight away. We started to decorate our flat, I resigned from work, and we started to pack our things to send home by ship. We felt very excited and you could see a brighter future for us in the Philippines. My last day at work turned out to be a very pleasant experience, although it was sad too. I knew I would miss the place and several of the people, but I was happy in my heart because this move was about our future as a family. I was pleasantly surprised because my manager had arranged a leaving party for me. I remember a friend saying, "Thank you for being a good friend to me." I was touched. Most of my work colleagues came and hugged and kissed me goodbye. They all thanked me for being a good friend, as well as a loyal work colleague. My manager presented me with an envelope full of money that they had collected for me. When I was on my way home on the train, I opened the envelope and I counted £300 they had generously given me! I was very grateful and straight away wrote them a thank you letter.

At home, I felt relieved knowing we were going home for good and I felt things would change for the better. Ven was still working at Greenwich Job Centre and was going to resign when we found a buyer for our flat. Sometimes Ven and I had lunch together; we

Chapter 7 - London, Jamaica, the Philippines; family travels

were very excited about our plans and I could see him getting desperate to leave his job. He was under a lot of pressure every day because of the management changes. Now I had time to look after Ven better and make sure he ate his lunch every day.

By January 2007, we had found a couple to buy our flat and I had to deal with everything. The only thing Ven needed to do was to sign the documents because the flat was in his name. We had so many things to get rid of and we gave most of them away. We had several send-off parties and these were happy moments for us because, although we would miss our friends, we were more excited about our new life in the Philippines.

However, we had many stressful moments before we left when time seemed to be against us! However, we got through all of these together and stayed our last night with Roger and Paula and it was lovely to see several of our business friends there that final night in England. Roger dropped us off at the airport the next day and I remember looking at Ven's face when we arrived at Heathrow Airport. He looked so relieved! When our plane eventually took off, I felt as though I was going to heaven! I had my immediate family with me and I was going to be near my extended family in the Philippines. Ven was over the moon as well. But JJ was not happy. He was sad at leaving England and it had been a struggle for him. We understood how he felt, but it was something we had to do and we had been very worried about JJ's future in England. The influences from outside were strong and we were not always there for him because of our work. We both wanted to spend more time with our son, and in the UK it wasn't possible because of the demands of our respective work.

77

You raise me up by Leila Wilks

Joe Marie's wedding

Joe Marie's wedding, with Joel, my father Luis, Abel and Jorge (from left to right)

Chapter 8 - The Philippines; a new life and new challenges

When we arrived in the Philippines, it took us a month to decide where to live. Prices were very high and we decided we needed to live in the house we were building, so we enrolled JJ in Corpus Christi High School, about ten minutes' walk away. JJ was the most miserable person at that time because he was struggling to adapt to his new environment. My family was very glad we lived near them now and they did their best to help JJ feel comfortable with our new situation. JJ learnt to speak our language very quickly with the help of his cousins, and soon he began to make friends at school. Ven walked him to school every day and met him after school in the afternoon. This made Ven very happy. We grew our business and we managed to put a big team together in a very short time.

We did all the things we had always wanted to do; helping people to grow their businesses and spending time with JJ. But five months after we arrived in the Philippines, something unexpected happened. One group in the business company in the UK messed things up. They did something against the law and it caused the company to carry out a serious investigation. They postponed business operations in the UK during the investigations, but it affected everyone in the company and many businesses all over the UK. At the end of the investigation, the company decided to make changes to the business operations. These were very unpopular with many people. We spoke to Roger and Paula, who told us they had decided not to do what the company had asked. We were devastated! The organisation we were in had nothing to do with the mess, but inevitably we were all affected. Ven and I could have continued building our business in the Philippines because we already had our local team there and it was growing quickly. For a week, we discussed it and asked several serious questions, but ultimately we decided to stop building it there. It was not an easy decision to make because there were many people involved.

It took us a while to pick up the courage to explain it to our team. Our leaders in the Philippines could not understand why we made this final decision. Our team leader Glory tried to get us to change our minds, but we couldn't. Ven and I started to look around to see if we could find something else we could do, a more conventional business.

On December 24th 2007, our first Christmas Eve in the Philippines, we had a family reunion. That day, Ven started having severe headaches all day. He said his neck and head felt hot. On Christmas Day at 6am, Ven passed out in the toilet. Luckily, I was there behind him. I called to my brothers and we took him directly to the Maria Reyna Hospital, one of the private hospitals in the city. Ven was being sick and the doctors were amazed at how strong he seemed despite his elevated blood pressure. Until this episode, Ven had been taking eight tablets a day, but after a week in hospital, the doctor increased his tablets to 12 a day. The doctor warned us that if he didn't continue to take the medication, he would have to go on dialysis.

We were very careful with his diet. He ate fish, vegetables and fruits, and drank large quantities of water every day. Ven sometimes mentioned things he desired to do, and I remember once, he said, "Before I die, I must have a goat farm."

Where my father came from in the province, there were people who raised goats and sold them to restaurant owners. This gave Ven an idea, and we decided to buy several highly-bred goats and several native goats to have a mixed breed flock. We heard of a guy in Alicomohan who was selling his native goats, so we drove there together and bought two. Uncle Isabelo looked after them for us, and one day he called to say that our female goat

Chapter 8 - The Philippines; a new life and new challenges

was pregnant. Ven was very excited about this and, of course, we were there when the goat was due. The mother goat, who Ven called Number One, had two babies, but I was not really keen on raising goats because I did not like them and they smelt unpleasant. However, I wanted Ven to be happy. When I saw the excitement in his eyes, it reminded me of when we started to build our business in England. Ven always needed to do something he was passionate about.

At this time, Roger in the UK shared with us a similar business concept to the one we had managed earlier. We always respected and valued his ideas because he had years of experience and expertise in this area. Without delay, we decided to do it as well. Ven was happy breeding his goats, so I went alone to Cebu to promote the new business venture, although meeting new people, which was critical for this type of business, was Ven's strength, not really mine. However, I took my niece, KC, to help me, and sometimes JJ came too.

One day, Uncle Isabelo said that their mayor in Sugbongcogon Town was selling high-breed goats from Australia. Ven was very interested to see them. We went to look at his goat farm where he raised different breeds. It was massive! Ven was very excited and we bought was a nice white male Anglo-Nubian goat, who Ven called Barako. He was as big as a calf!

Ven also wanted to buy a piece of land to build a goat house so we could have more, perhaps as many as 100 goats, and run a business selling them to the restaurant owners.

We went to Alicomohan to see Uncle Isabelo, and he offered to sell us a piece of land near his house, where we started to build our goat house. It took us more than a month, and in the meantime we bought more native goats, and we bred more too. By the time we finished building the goat house, we had eight goats, and I had started to actually like them! They are lovely animals and harmless. Ven talked to them and gave them all names. As soon as they saw Ven coming, they came together as if they wanted to be with their father. They all gathered around him and Ven stroked them one by one.

At his new school, JJ was slowly getting used to the environment, especially when he started to play football. They played football matches in Pelaiz Sports Centre, and every morning I took JJ there for practice. When JJ played in a football tournament, Ven came to support him and JJ said his dad was his number one fan that day. When JJ scored, Ven ran onto the field and gave him a big hug! JJ still talks about the times he spent with his dad at those weekends as the happiest moments of his life. Otherwise, at the weekends, Ven, JJ and I went to the goat house. JJ grew to like them too. I had an idea to raise pigs and we asked Uncle Isabelo if we could use his empty pigsty, which he agreed. We started with two high-breed pigs, who produced piglets very quickly, which we kept for three months before selling them.

On April 27th 2008, Ven celebrated his 54th birthday. I went to buy him a surprise birthday present, a healthy, brown, high-breed Anglo-Nubian, and I called her 54. It was hard to hide the goat from him because of the goat noises, but I gave it to him at his birthday party and he was delighted! Ven had invited a young lady to his party who I did not know. He had learnt how to use a mobile phone and he enjoyed communicating with friends and started to explore meeting new people again, mostly women! He found it fascinating to be able to communicate with anyone he felt like contacting, though he probably didn't realise that several women had ulterior motives. We had a great time at the party. Ven enjoyed dancing with my sister Enesia and playing his reggae music and he was very happy that day. When JJ and I showed him the goat, he cried and said, "It is precious, thanks so much," and he gave me a big hug.

Chapter 8 - The Philippines; a new life and new challenges

Ven had also invited a few other women from his weekly reflexology group. He loved that group and it was good for his health. We invited our new friends, Steve and Helen Wallis, and their daughter Katrina. Helen was eight months' pregnant. Ven and I had met Helen on the boat going home from one of our trips to Cebu City. Helen was passing Cagayan on her way home from seeing Steve off to England at Mactan Airport Cebu. Ven started to talk about football and asked what team Steve supported. We found out that Steve used to live with a Jamaican family and he knew all about Jamaica, especially when it came to music. Knowing this, Ven knew he would have a good friend there and that was how our friendship started. After that, we went to see them on a regular basis and they visited us every time they came to Cagayan.

Ven became more active and started to play tennis again, every day, and he went to see the goats at the weekend. He was meeting people everywhere he went and it was good for him. He walked JJ to school every morning and then walked on to the tennis court near the Cathedral Church, where he had met most of his tennis partners.

By this time, our family business consisted of 22 goats, two motorelas and one multi-cab in Cebu. Ven was taking 12 tablets a day to keep his blood pressure under control and to save his one working kidney. No one would have known he had a health problem because he was very happy and active. However, we were still not earning as much money as we needed because we had to spend 22,000 pesos a month on Ven's maintenance tablets. We kept these problems to ourselves. Ven told me not to buy so many of the tablets and he would be fine, but I continued to buy them because I was concerned that he might have to go on dialysis. There was a time when he would intentionally miss taking his medicine because he knew we were hard up for money. He wanted to raise more goats so we could start to sell them to restaurants. We continued to breed them with Barako, who

83

looked dangerous with his big horns! We had to buy the right food for the high-breed goats. We usually bought the goat food from the town in Salay every two weeks. I did not see the point in going so frequently, so Ven went alone. He caught the bus and met my nephew Ronillo in the goat feed shop. Ven enjoyed travelling by bus and he talked to the drivers and soon most of the bus drivers for Balingoan knew him. Meanwhile, I continued running our marketing business and sharing information with Roger and Paula in the UK. I also tried to contact people from our previous business. Ven took our business flyers and magazines with him and showed them to the new people he met. For about six months, we operated separately like this and I left it with Ven and Ronillo to take care of the goats and the pigs. Occasionally, I went to see the animals but Ven seemed happy and enjoyed what he was doing very much.

One day, I had a strange feeling inside me, which I didn't understand. I was cleaning the house and I had strong feeling directing me to climb up to the top of Ven's turntable on the record player. It was something I had never done in the past but there was an urgency I had never felt before. As soon as I lifted the turntable, I saw Ven's bank book. I was curious because he never hid anything from me and I was puzzled as to why he had put it there. When I opened it, I saw he had been making regular withdrawals and that the money was nearly finished in his account. I saw the dates of his withdrawals and they were twice a week but I always gave him the money to buy the goat and pig food. Ven had enough money for the bus fare and to buy himself food when he went there. Ven would normally talk to me about everything he was doing and we always discussed things together before making any decisions. I worked hard that day not to be upset about what I had discovered, but my emotions took control and as soon as he came home, I asked if he had started another project without telling me.

"No," he said.

Chapter 8 - The Philippines; a new life and new challenges

I hid his bank book and started studying his moves. I noticed that he took his mobile phone with him everywhere, including to the bathroom where I heard him talking to someone. One morning, he forgot to take his phone with him and I heard a text message come in. I picked up the phone and read the message: "Good morning, babe!"

I was fuming with anger and called to him and asked him who this person was.

He said, "It's only a friend," and straight away grabbed his phone from me and left the house.

We had builders who were working on the small apartment we were building to rent out. Ven stayed out there the whole day sending texts to people and talking on the phone. That afternoon, my sister Enesia from Alicomohan came to see me and she asked me if Ven was training a young lady for our new business.

"No," I said, "why do you ask?"

She said Ven had taken a young lady to our goat house and introduced her as his business student. They had gone to Sugbongcogon and had lunch together in the restaurant and did not come back to the goat house. It suddenly dawned on me that whenever Ven went to the goat house, he always came home late. Everything was becoming clearer to me now without searching for an answer to his unusual attitude. I did not tell anyone about the bank book and the text message; I kept it to myself.

My nephew Ronillo decided to stop looking after the goats and I employed a cousin from Carmen Agusan to work with the goats. I continued to monitor Ven and I asked my cousin to text me when he arrived in the goat house and when he left. Sure enough, he always left the goat house at 2pm but didn't get home until after 8pm, and it was only a one and a half hour bus ride.

85

I concluded that my husband was seeing somebody on a regular basis. I asked Enesia to describe the lady to me and it was the same lady he had invited to his 54th birthday party. I knew he had contacted this lady to join our new business, but I was now sure he had gone too far with the relationship, and I cried like a baby! I had never had this experience in our 15 years of marriage and I didn't know what to do.

At first, I felt like hitting him! But then inside I felt I wanted to be nice to him so he would stop what he was doing. I worked hard to keep the angry feeling inside me. One evening I asked him in a nice way where did he normally go after seeing the goats. He suddenly got angry with me for asking the question.

"Are you trying to say I am being dishonest with you?" he replied.

I repeated the question, but it quickly became a strong argument between us and I ended up shouting at him. "If you want to be with someone else, be honest with me!"

He was angry and said he would never have an affair with anyone and if I didn't believe him, it was my problem.

I cried and asked him why he had turned this way.

But he didn't answer my question.

He was angry with me most of the time and we had a communication breakdown. We were both angry with each other and we behaved like two strangers in the house, which was a very painful situation to experience because we had been so close.

One evening, he came home and went straight to bed. In our bedroom drawer, I found one of the business folders he always carried with him and inside one of the business magazines, I saw, written by him, the name of a hotel, date and time booked ahead. I was fuming after seeing it! I woke him up and asked him who he was meeting in this hotel. He denied it and said it was not for him, but that made me angrier and I said to him, "I do not want to have a husband who is seeing another woman. If you want to leave me, go! Or if you don't, I will go."

JJ woke up and heard our argument.

In the morning, I talked to JJ, but he refused to believe that his dad would do such a thing. JJ thought I was being suspicious.

The next day, I packed my clothes; I was desperate to go far away and be on my own. Ven called JJ and they talked together. When I was leaving, they walked with me to the bus terminal and they took the bus with me. I went to a hotel in Gingoog City, and JJ and Ven were there with me. I stopped talking to them and kept to myself.

On the date he had written down about the hotel, we were together in the hotel in Gingoog City. Ven and JJ spent time together, and I was alone and very quiet. We were there together but as a miserable family. I could not take in the fact that my husband had another woman. I was in tears every day and kept asking myself why he had turned out this way. Ven continued talking to me until I responded. Eventually we were able to talk without getting angry.

I asked him, "Why have you changed and why have you looked at other women? Do you not love me anymore?"

"I never had anyone in my life aside from you, since we got married," Ven replied.

But I didn't believe him. His actions spoke louder than his words. I could not believe or trust him anymore, and I called him a liar! I stopped calling him "Darling" and I smashed his phone in front of him and took out the sim card.

He had erased all the text messages but when I put it in my phone, I saw a lady had sent him a text asking to meet him in a restaurant. I rang the number but she did not answer. I felt as though the sky had fallen in on me!

My life was suddenly very dark and miserable, and I felt all the happiness had been taken away from me. I said to him, "Leave me and we will sell everything we have and share it between us."

I said these things every day to him but the more I said it, the more he wanted to stay. I wanted to give him the freedom because I felt maybe he would be happier with a younger lady. I had convinced myself he did not love me anymore, because at that time I had gained weight and did not feel good about myself.

I was surprised my relatives hadn't told me they had seen Ven with this lady a few times. When I asked them, they said they thought it was ok with me because Ven had introduced her to them as our business student. The same lady came to our house a few times and Ven had talked to her about our business and I had left Ven with her discussing work. One day a cousin said to me, "There is another lady in the goat and pig food shop who Ven has exchanged phone numbers with. He meets her outside and they talk and have fun and laugh." He said Ven liked this other lady and had given her money. So now I learnt it was more than one lady, and I felt very hurt and intimidated! The lady at the goat feed shop was only 19 years old, and the other one was 27, and it made me feel all the more hurt and miserable. I started to blame myself for being too trusting of Ven.

Chapter 8 - The Philippines; a new life and new challenges

Glorecita Tan (Glory) and I in 2007

Ven, Jorge, Steve, myself and Katrina (Helen's older daughter)

You raise me up by Leila Wilks

Uncle Isabelo, myself, Enesia, Nellie, my father Luis, and Kenneth

Chapter 9 - The Philippines; goats, pigs and public transport

One morning, Ven asked if he could have a word with me. I ignored him so he sat down and wrote a letter to me. I was doing a lot of thinking and reading as many positive books as I could. I had re-read *Tough Times Never Last, but Tough People Do* by Robert H. Schuller. I cried, read and cried. Ven's CD *Stand Up For Jesus* had helped me to cling to God. I played that CD day and night. It took me a while to have the peace of mind to talk to Ven but he said that to remove my doubts about him, I should start again going with him wherever he went. He had decided he didn't want to have a mobile phone anymore and I should stop worrying about him having an affair with someone.

I decided to do this so when he went to the tennis court to play, I sat there and watched, although I was still unhappy because I felt I could not trust him anymore. My mind was always in doubt about my husband. I had an unforgiving heart towards him because I kept imagining how he had betrayed me. I had all these negative emotions and thoughts running in my mind every day. I felt very sorry for myself and I was like a child who had their toys taken away from them. Although I could see how hard Ven tried to put things right, we still did not have peace at home.

One day he asked me to go with him to visit the goats and I refused. I continued monitoring him to see if he had stopped seeing the ladies. I asked my cousin to send me a text when he arrived at the goat house and when he left. When he was due to come home, I went to the bus terminal. When I saw him, I followed him as he walked towards the shops. I saw that he rang someone from a public phone because I was across the road watching him. I lost control as soon as I saw him talking to someone on the phone. I went straight to him, grabbed the phone and heard a woman laughing at the other end. I was very angry again. I slapped him and was crying and shouting at the same time. When we got home, he spoke to JJ and I heard him explain that Mum and Dad weren't getting on well any more. JJ came to me and said in a harsh voice, "You are too jealous!" He ran away from home that night and his cousins went out looking for him. It was a troubled night for us all. I went to our room and continued crying. I played *Stand Up For Jesus* to comfort me.

In our neighbourhood, everyone could hear our fights. A few people came to me and said they had seen Ven with this lady a few times but they did not want to get involved. I was very hurt and confused because Ven had never done these kinds of things before. I started to wonder if something was wrong with him or me, mentally. Our future plan had gone out of the window and no matter how I worked it out in my head, I was really hurting and feeling tortured deep inside me.

I rang Roger and Paula and told them everything. They were not happy and wanted to talk to Ven but he would not talk to them. He became even more annoyed with me because I told them what had happened. I started to go to church again and asked God what was happening in my life. Why, all of a sudden, had these troubles and burdens come to me? I had stopped talking to Ven again, but at least I was praying quietly to God. I started going to church every day, and I asked God why Ven had changed completely and was like a stranger to me.

I had heard many stories about families who went home, as we had done, and the husband had left his wife and children to run away with a helper; or families who had separated because the husband had found a younger woman. It seemed very common in the Philippines where many women simply wanted to get money from a man and they didn't care when a family was destroyed.

Chapter 9 - The Philippines; goats, pigs and public transport

I thought back to when I went to see a solicitor about buying into the public transport business. She had asked me why we had come home. She said, "Is England not good enough? There is nothing here!"

She said it was not a wise idea to come home to my country because it was very rare that a family would last long together. She talked about families who were separated because husbands had affairs with other women. But at the time, I had ignored her. A friend told me that many local women are so desperate to find a foreigner, they don't care if the man is married. Knowing these things now, I began to realise how big the temptation was for Ven every day when he was out on his own. Temptations only a very strong and wise person can overcome without destroying their marriage. The best thing I had done was to smash Ven's phone because he did not buy another one.

I needed to make a serious decision.

I had never thought that women would be a temptation for Ven because in our previous business, we dealt with many younger women and Ven treated them as though they were his sisters! Ven had stopped using our bedroom and slept upstairs next to JJ's room. Months passed and I slowly got hold of myself and decided to do something to change our circumstances.

It was another turning point in my life.

I spoke to Ven and suggested we asked for forgiveness from each other for everything we have done against one another.

From that time, if I didn't go with him when he went out, he stayed at home. At last we started to treat each other in the way we used to. A friend came to visit us from England and we took her to Camiguin and White Island, which were so beautiful and we had a great time.

It felt as though nothing challenging had happened in my life so recently.

Ven and I had decided to focus on our goats and pigs project and we spent most of our time on this together. They were breeding, but every week a kid or a piglet died so we went to find a veterinarian to see how we could prevent these deaths happening. Uncle Isabelo had a veterinarian friend who came to the goat house and helped us sort out this problem. He taught us how to keep an eye on the small ones and feed the mother with the right food during their pregnancy and after the delivery. I was very happy when Ven and I started to do things together again and to plan for our future again, together.

Ven had met a few minibus owners and drivers and became interested in the public transport business, and we decided to run a public transport business in Cebu City. Most of the family could drive so we bought a ten-seater vehicle called a multi-cab, which my brother Abel and his wife Nila drove for us. Back at our home in Cagayan de Oro City, we bought an eight-seater Mitsubishi Adventure. Ven really liked this vehicle and viewed it as part of his family. He called it Ade! He looked after it himself and my brother Jorge drove it for us. Ven said he would never drive in the Philippines because of the crazy way people drove in my country. We decided to use our ten-seater Mitsubishi Adventure to drive the four-hour trip from our city to Butuan City.

We also invested in a motorela, which is a local motorbike attached to a carriage at the back that carries six people. Ven enjoyed riding in these vehicles and they always made him laugh. He found it cute, but also a good way to earn a living. Ven painted a creative design on it, yellow and red, and it looked beautiful! It was one of the prettiest designs running in the City and Ven was very happy.

Chapter 9 - The Philippines; goats, pigs and public transport

Then Ven wanted the designer to print positive, inspirational quotes on the motorela, phrases like, "*If you think you can, you can*" and "*If you are going through hell, keep going*".

Many people rode on our moterela and took notes of the quotes. It became very popular. We invested in three motorelas to drive in the city with hired drivers and we started to earn good money every day. But then we needed to finance the goat project and Ven's daily medication. By now, JJ had settled into his school and starting to enjoy his life, making new friends and playing football competitively. He also formed a band with his musical friends, and Ven and I were very happy to see our son settled.

Life improved for us during this period, but Ven and I knew we still had many problems to overcome. Ven liked to meet and help people. He did not think about himself. The neighbourhood and street children loved Ven, and they listened to him speaking with signs, which I had to interpret because they did not understand him. Ven asked me to teach him the local language so he could speak with them. Several of these children understood Ven because they went to school and learnt English. We decided to teach them about God and they gathered together once a week and KC, my niece, taught them to pray.

One day, Ven said, "I would love to build a home for the street children and orphans."

I agreed and said, "Let's do it! When our personal finances are in order, we will build them a home."

He continued, "I would feel very happy to see them off the street. We can teach them to speak English so that they can understand me and can communicate with foreigners."

Early in 2009, we tried out the minibus run. We planned to do it for a month and then buy a larger one if it worked. We hired a driver and we soon had a full service every time. Ven and I went with the driver and collected the money ourselves because we didn't feel able to trust the driver fully. Ven set up a system in our vehicle so he could play his collection of music and everyone enjoyed their journeys with us! Ven's reggae music was inspirational Gospel songs by Osmond Collins, such as *"He Will Restore"*.

Ven played his music while we were in the bus terminal as well as on the bus, and everyone loved it. We also played a music collection Roger had sent us, a great collection from various artists, and we knew all the tracks and loved listening to them together. They were happy days and, best of all, I had my husband back!

We ran the bus at night because it was a trial and we did not have a license yet. Although we fully intended to act honestly, we were wrong and, sure enough, one morning, 30 minutes away from the bus terminal, we were stopped by the police. They asked for our papers, which we did not have. We had to ask all the passengers to transfer to the regular bus to finish their journey and we gave them back their fares. It was a very embarrassing moment for us both. The police took away our Mitsubishi Adventure and they gave us a fine to claim it back. Ven felt very annoyed because he knew there were so many minibus owners who ran their businesses without a franchise who had survived for years!

However, Ven and I decided to do the right thing. We sold our Mitsubishi Adventure and, months later, bought an 18-seater second-hand red minibus. Ven called it Super Red. It was a hard decision to make because we were attached to our Adventure, but we wanted to earn money the right way. It was a long process to put the new minibus on the road. We had to pass many tests and the franchise processing involved a long wait. We also faced many challenges setting up this business. I was told that one of our motorela drivers had taken the original parts out of our

Chapter 9 - The Philippines; goats, pigs and public transport

motorela and replaced them with local ones so he could sell the original parts. We parked all the motorelas beside the driver's house because although where we first lived had a big space to park vehicles, one day a rich man from outside the city bought the whole area and built a wall around it to run his truck business. We did not have any warning and when we appealed, no one was interested in hearing our case. Most house owners simply had their piece of land with enough space for their house to stand on, but because they didn't own vehicles, it did not bother them. We had a problem parking our vehicles safely and now this driver had abused our trust by his actions. I had to control my temper because I knew it was not worth getting angry and shouting at him. I called him to our house and asked where these parts were. We took our motorela and had it checked and we found that all the original parts were missing. The driver was very proud and wouldn't admit what he had done. He became very angry and refused to drive for us anymore. It was obvious he was guilty but was covering it up.

Ven and I had to find a new driver quickly and we found an expert who had the ability to fix the motorela if something went wrong with it. His name was Ross and he had eight children to feed so we knew we had a long-term driver here, and he soon became part of our family. Ven and I found a piece of land to rent and we built a garage for our vehicles to be safe. Ven and the drivers used to stay there sometimes to clean our vehicles, and Ven loved to stay in the garage in the evenings and listen to his music. I had noticed a helper across from the garage was friendly with Ven, who of course loved chatting to everyone, but soon these two became very friendly towards each other. The garage was five minutes' walk away from our house and my nieces told me that they saw him every morning. I did not want to follow him all the time because I thought those days were over. However, I soon noticed that he was there every morning saying he was going to listen to music and clean the vehicle, even when it didn't need cleaning! Whenever we saw the lady walking on the road and we were inside the vehicle, he purposely didn't look at her, as though they didn't know one another. I questioned Ven and he began to behave strangely again, not wanting to talk to me. I asked him why this was happening again, but he ignored me and said I was the one behaving badly. I started to get confused and felt empty. I realised Ven was not the same person again towards me. He began behaving like a stranger. I became very depressed and discouraged about my life again but I said to myself I needed to do whatever I could to save our marriage. I cried every day and wished Roger and Paula were near because I knew they would understand and listen to my struggles. I kept these feelings hidden from my family because I did not want them to see the full extent of what I was experiencing and I did not want them to hate Ven.

Our friend Steve came to visit his family, Helen and the children. Ven and I were the godparents to their daughter, Marley. Every time Steve was around, we went to visit them. They lived near the tennis court Ven had joined. Someone told me that one of the tennis ladies had caused two families to break up by having an affair with their foreign husbands. She had a record of breaking relationships, and I was very concerned about this. I always watched them play and was very jealous. However, I did not leave Ven on his own with her, which was very uncomfortable for everyone. I had started to smoke again, which upset Ven because he hated me to smoke. He shouted at me to stop, but I continued secretly. We were always annoyed with each other at this time because I smoked and he got close to these women of which I was bitterly jealous.

One morning, I decided to see a priest in our church and he said I should go to church every day and pray to a particular statue of a saint and things would be all right. He said he would also pray for me. I told him everything that I had experienced since coming back to the Philippines with my family from England. He told me to give money to the church on a regular basis in an envelope and continue to pray. However, life got worse after that

Chapter 9 - The Philippines; goats, pigs and public transport

and I did not understand why. The priest referred me to a nun and I went to see her on a regular basis, but nothing changed. Our goats and pigs were dying and the new vehicle we bought in Cebu, which my brother Abel ran, kept breaking down.

The motorelas were breaking down as well and we were always spending money on them. Ven and I ended up selling the one Ross was driving because it was breaking down every week. However, I found out that our driver on the new motorela was running it day and night without our permission. He had asked if he could park it at his home and he would look after it. We discovered he was making more money than we were because people reported to us that he was driving it at night although he would never admit that he did. He was only allowed to drive it in the day because we did not want to overuse it. Of course, he kept the money for himself apart from the money on the days he was working for us. This man had always seemed to us very trustworthy and he was serious when it came to his job. He worked hard to earn money for his family and we respected him. His wife was very friendly with us and we felt comfortable with his family. It was not easy to handle this situation, but then I knew the people who saw him driving at night were close to me and I knew they would not lie to me. I am not a firm person, so I felt uneasy dealing with it, but Ven insisted I had to stop it as soon as possible. As we had sold the other motorela, Ross had lost his job and we wanted him to take over because he seemed very honest and loyal to us.

One morning, the driver of our new motorela asked us for money to buy a new tyre, but I was warned by one of the other motorela owners that most drivers would buy a second-hand tyre if we gave them the money and it would be wiser to buy them ourselves! We had always asked for a receipt but these drivers had been around for a long time and they knew people who could provide receipts. Another day, that same driver had an accident when he was driving, which was his fault, but because we were the owners

99

of the vehicle, we had to pay the victim, plus we needed to spend money to fix the damage. We realised we had to fire him. I tried hard to talk to him nicely but firmly and told him we couldn't afford having all these things happening regularly. He would have to find another motorela to drive. He could not believe what he heard. He was obviously hoping everything would continue as normal and he was very annoyed. The next day, his wife came and asked me if we could give him more time because she insisted what had happened was not his fault. I was firm this time and refused to keep him. Since that day, they stopped talking to us and completely avoided us.

Ven and JJ eating sugar cane

Chapter 9 - The Philippines; goats, pigs and public transport

Ven and our goat Barako, the breeder

Ven and our goats

Ven & JJ with Steve & Helen in Marley's christening (Helen and Steve's daughter)

Ven and me at Marley's christening (Helen and Steve's daughter)

Chapter 10 - The Philippines; dealing with unknown demons

Someone said to me, "It looks as though you have been cursed and you should really consider checking it out."

I did not believe in these things. I thought we did not have any enemies. We were nice people who believed in working hard. We had helped a lot of people and we never wanted to hurt anyone.

But we were told, "Some people are very jealous of you and they don't want you to succeed and live happily."

I told Ven and he didn't believe it either, but when things started getting worse, we wondered if we needed to do something about it. We had become close again and I saw how much it hurt Ven when the goats died. I went back to the priest and continued to pray in front of the saint's statue inside the church, but this didn't help and I realised that it was God I wanted to connect with, although at that time I didn't know how to. I cried my heart out asking for help, but our lives became worse.

I suddenly felt the urge to go to Carmen where my mother's brother lived and I told Ven I needed to follow up this idea. I went there on my own by bus, and when I arrived, I told Uncle Democrito and Aunty Estelita about what was happening in my life. Aunty Estelita referred me to a palm reader who was able to undo a witchcraft.

The next day, I went with Uncle Democrito on a motorbike to a very remote area of Carmen, and I was scared! We went to a small chapel, where there was a big statue of the Mother Mary and other saints. The person we saw was well known for his ability to achieve unusual things and also for his healing powers, and the small chapel was packed with other people. We were told to buy a bunch of candles from his small shop in front of the chapel. We wrote down our names on a paper and joined a long queue. When my turn came, I explained briefly what had happened and he asked me to write down the names of people I thought were annoyed with my husband and I, people who would intentionally hurt us for any reason. When I handed the list of five names to him, he placed it on the altar, together with the other peoples' lists. He sat in front of us and played his guitar and we sang together. This man was known to make a thief return what he had stolen because his whole body itched until he returned the stolen goods. I had never seen so many candles in my life. Everyone around us was praying and lighting candles. Something strange happened after he had prayed. People lined up in front of him and he pricked the side of their heads with his fingers. We did not see a needle, but when he placed his fingers on our heads, it felt like a needle pricking. After the prayers, he called us again one by one to the front to tell us what the problem was. When he called me, he took my list and pointed to three of the names on it. According to him, these people were using witchcraft to destroy me, my husband, my son and our health. I was shocked when I saw the names and didn't want to believe it.

I asked him what would happen next, and he said, "If you do not take defensive action, it will completely destroy you and your family."

He gave me a list of things to buy if I decided to continue, and I went home very distressed and confused. These things I needed to buy were not free and I told Ven all about it. Ven and I did not want to believe it because we were used to doing things fairly and not worry about anyone else. It had not crossed our minds there might be people who wanted to destroy our lives.

I was not sure about it, so I told Ven I wanted to see a different person and see what they would say. I went to see a woman

Chapter 10 - The Philippines; dealing with unknown demons

who was well known for doing the same sort of thing, and she too asked me to write down names of people who would possibly want to hurt us. I made out the same list of names and strangely enough she picked the same names again. Ven and I started to think it might be true, but inside me, I was not sure. I looked for yet another person far away from the previous ones because I thought maybe these people knew one another and had communicated with each other. I went to two other people in the same field, and again they picked exactly the same names.

At last, we decided we needed to act on this so I went back to the first healer. When we arrived, he was delighted to meet Ven because he was the first foreigner he had helped. He and Ven became friends straight away! We made a commitment to go there once a week and we paid him money, and in return he gave us stuff to place around the house, to form a protection against the work of the witchcraft. He also told us that Ven's changed attitude, previously to me, had been due to the witchcraft too. It was on track to destroy our marriage and everything we owned. We did everything he said to stop these things happening and sure enough, shortly after that, the goats and the pigs stopped dying. In fact, we had multiplied the numbers of goats again from 22 to 33, and Ven and I were happy once more.

But on March 21st 2009, Ven suddenly said to me, "I can't hear what you are talking about. I can't hear anything."

Slowly, he felt weaker and weaker and was slipping off the seat. We rushed him to a private hospital because I had learnt from our previous experiences that in an emergency, we needed to see a private doctor quickly. At the Polymedic Hospital, we found out that Ven's blood pressure was very high and he had suffered a mild stroke. He was kept there for a week, and although we did not have much money, I had to make sure he got the right treatment. I was very worried and scared that something would happen to him. I was glad our friend Steve was in the country at that time and I was able to borrow money from him for Ven's medical treatment.

I rang Roger and Paula and told them what had happened. Every day that Ven was in the hospital, he had to have a very expensive injection. The bills started to add up every day, plus there was a daily charge for the room. I rang the healer and explained we are in the hospital and he said he would pray for us. I started to borrow money from lending companies. When Ven was discharged after a week, we had to pay a bill of almost 10,000 pesos, which was approximately £200 in those days!

Ven had to rest and recover after this episode, while I continued to manage the minibus franchise we had now acquired. After this hospital experience, we were hard up for money, and Ven and I discussed what we should do. I wanted to stop raising goats but I knew the happiness they gave Ven. He spent days feeding the goats, walking with them in the field where there was grass for them to eat. It was amazing how the goats knew Ven like their father. As soon as they heard Ven's voice calling their names, they responded bleating running towards him. It was an amazing to watch and yet no one had trained them. Ven took jackfruit leaves with him and the goats loved it and surrounded him to eat them. When the goats were fed, Roberto, who took care of them for us, took the goats into their little rooms and they sat there quietly. Ven could stand and watch them for hours. Certainly the goats were pretty and they looked very healthy. One of the female goats looked like a Dalmatian dog and Ven called her Honey. She had borne babies twice already. Barako, the male goat, was also handsome and healthy too.

Ven gradually regained normal health and continued his regular medication. We had borrowed more money and put up our house as collateral to continue the goat project, though it did not make sense to me to carry on like this. I tried to persuade Ven to start selling the goats, but he said it was not the right time yet.

Chapter 10 - The Philippines; dealing with unknown demons

Honey bore two more kid goats, and on my birthday Ven bought me a lovely white Anglo-Nubian goat as my present. She was spotless, as white as snow, and Ven called her Snowy. It was a special thing for me from my husband. I felt very happy that day.

However, I was very concerned about our financial situation, and Ven's medication bills were my biggest concern. At this stage of our lives, Ven and I were happy again, as we used to be, but deep inside I was very worried about his health. My brother Jorge and Ross continued to run the motorelas and earn a small income for us every day, which covered our daily food and JJ's school projects. Sometimes Ven went for a ride in the motorelas, and we were also running our 18-seater minibus. We did short journeys at first and my brother Jorge drove it for us while I was the conductor collecting the fare, and I really enjoyed it and was proud to do it!

One day, we needed to buy a special feed for the pregnant goats, but I realised we did not have enough money, so I pawned my necklace and wedding ring. The following week, we needed to go back to see the goats because they had babies. Two of the goats had two babies each in two days. I started thinking of what else I could pawn so we could buy special feed for the mothers. I decided to pawn our Sony video camera, the one we brought back from England, and we managed to buy the feed that day, but of course, the next month I needed to find the money to collect my necklace and ring from the pawn shop. Ven's money from the UK was the only money we were relying on for JJ's monthly school fees, Ven's monthly medication and our monthly bills. We started to struggle to pay JJ's monthly tuition and went to ask the school director to sign a promissory note so JJ would be able to attend his exams. The school director was very strict when it came to school payments and there was always a long queue to see him because many parents were in the same position as us.

Once when the school director would not sign the promissory note, I cried and explained our position. Slowly he reached out his pen to sign it. I felt very distant from the world that day and as if there was no one to help us. I felt utterly lost! I went home and talked to Ven about everything and cried. We went to see Helen and Steve and told them about our visits to the healer and what he was doing for us. Helen did not believe in that kind of thing, but I felt relieved that we had actually talked to someone else about it. I did not like to share it with Roger and Paula because I thought it would have been too strange for them to understand. I am not a person to go around complaining about my life, and Ven was the same. Ven and I always talked about what else we could do to change the situation, but we felt things were happening out of our control. We said to each other that we must never give up.

One morning, we needed to buy feed again for the goats so Ven said he would ring a close family friend in England. I did not want to ask for help from anyone, but we had to. We went to a public international call service and he made the call. He tried to explain our position and asked for financial help, but I could see the disappointment in his face and the conversation ended abruptly. We could not go to see the goats that week because we did not have the money to buy their food. Even though we struggled financially, I made sure Ven had his medication every day. The doctor had warned us to make sure he took the tablets on a regular basis, otherwise he would have to go on dialysis and that would be even more costly.

Ven and I helped the canvassers to get passengers for our minibus, but we had a quiet season for several months and we could hardly fill a load. We decided to run it to Valencia Bukidnon, which was further up from our city. This involved leaving in the night and getting back early in the morning in time to pick up other passengers. We thought of many things we could do and where to run the minibus because we were not making money out of it

Chapter 10 - The Philippines; dealing with unknown demons

at this time. I started to regret having a minibus because although it could do long journeys, we could hardly afford the petrol. At last, Ven said we needed to sell some of the goats and I was able to pay the pawn shops and recover my ring and necklace.

Ven liked to stay in the terminus, washing his minibus, playing his music, dancing about, and being happy and content! We hired a new driver but we wouldn't leave him to run it on his own because we felt we needed to collect the fares ourselves. We had learnt from our previous experience that drivers did not always tell us the whole story of where they went if left on their own! Most of the minibus owners drove their minibuses themselves for this reason, but Ven was not prepared to drive it himself and he was right because there were always accidents happening and most of them were fatal.

At this stage, Ven and I were fairly happy because we were doing things together and we both liked to travel. We called ourselves 'The Travellers' because we liked to see different places. For me, most of all, I felt that my husband was the same person again and I had him back! The money we earned from the minibus journeys was a great help towards paying for Ven's medication, JJ's school fees and our bank loan.

Every time we travelled in the minibus, we passed lovely places and Ven commented on how pretty the mountains were, the rice fields and the sea. We often drove near the seaside and, coming home from Butuan City, we watched the sunset. We would look at each other and Ven said, "This is a memory that we will carry with us forever."

I remember wishing that JJ was with us to see this beauty too. One Saturday, we were able to take JJ with us for the ride while taking passengers at the same time. We arrived back in our city late that evening having seen the sunset again, this time with JJ. It had given Ven the opportunity to show JJ all the nice places that we often saw on our journeys. I always remember that evening as a great happy moment for the three of us.

We had so many problems with dishonest drivers that after a while, Ven and I left the responsibility for running the minibus with my nephew, Randy. We trusted him and Ven and I wanted to focus on the goats and pigs. The vet came twice a month to check our animals and give us instructions about what to do and buy for them. The goats and pigs continued to multiply and it seemed two were doing well, but financially things were not good. I suggested to Ven again and again we needed to stop the animal project because we could not keep up with the expense of looking after them. But Ven did not agree with me. He said, "When we have 50 goats, we can start to sell them," but I was not sure we would ever get to that many goats in a reasonable time.

Chapter 11 - The Philippines; health and financial crises

I continued to go to church every Sunday, and hearing words from the Bible was very helpful to me. Ven and JJ came with me on a regular basis. However, one day I had a serious asthma attack, which meant I had to spend more money to buy medication for me this time! I decided not to stay in the hospital but rested at home and used a nebuliser on a regular basis. Fortunately, my sister Jennelisa had one already. It was the fireworks' smoke that triggered off the asthma. Around about this time, our bus in Cebu City, which my brother Abel was running, kept having regular breakdowns on their journeys, which meant we were spending more money than we were earning. We decided to sell it, but we got much less for it than we had originally bought it for. With this money, we managed to pay off a few of our debts and JJ's school fees.

One day, Ven and I went to visit our animals and we took a month's supply of the food for them. We asked Ross to drive us and, although the weather was not good that day, we had to go. On our return, we encountered a flood, where everyone had to evacuate and leave their homes. My brother Jorge and his wife Richel, their children and the rest of my family were helping each other and brought our possessions upstairs. The water had been to their waists, but by the time we arrived, the water had gone down. However, we were instructed to leave our home because there were more flood waters predicted due to a big storm in our area. With the family help, we took all our vehicles to the upper side of our area and we tried to sleep in our vehicles, though this was nearly impossible because there were many mosquitoes in the area.

The next night, we had to park our vehicles inside the local school campus. Most people sheltered inside the school and the Barangay Centre, while Ven, JJ and I stayed inside our vehicles. The rain did not stop and the water rose again. Most of the men went to their homes to find food and bring more possessions, but I asked Ven to stay with us. We were there for a week until the storm stopped. It was fortunate we had the vehicles and the drivers were able to continue to work during the day. We lived in the lower part of the area for a long time and never knew it was a flood risk area before. It was a horrible experience for all of us, and in this flood we lost many of our treasured family photographs.

In March 2010, Ven started to feel very weak and was having terrible headaches. One morning, he struggled to breathe and watching him struggle, I did not think about money. We decided to rush him to a private hospital and I called the family and asked them to find Jorge or Ross to take Ven on the motorela. Ven was attended by two doctors when we arrived at the hospital, and later we found out he'd had a heart attack. His blood pressure was very high and his lungs were full of water and he needed quick treatment. When I look back, it seems strange to me that the same month in the previous year, he was confined to hospital because he had a stroke. While we were in the hospital, on top of the heart attack, he had another stroke. That night, we all thought he was going to die. JJ had joined us in the hospital with his cousins and I went home because I needed to think and cry. I did not know what to do and I cried to God for help. I needed to prepare Ven's clothes to take to the hospital because I knew he would be there a long time. After one week in the hospital, Ven needed an injection a day to keep his blood pressure down, but a week later, Ven did not wake up! We called the doctor and they did everything to rouse him. I suppose Ven's body was shocked with the high dosage of medication. Again, we thought he would die that night and I was very scared.

Chapter 11 - The Philippines; health and financial crises

Eventually, he did wake up, and it was funny because he was annoyed with the doctor who had slapped him on his face so many times. However, as soon as Ven knew he had to have all this medicine, he demanded they stop giving it to him.

He shouted at the doctor, "I want you to send me home! I don't want to stay here!"

The doctor ignored him and talked to me instead. He said Ven's situation was very serious and we needed to put him on dialysis. After the doctor left, I explained everything to Ven, and he said to me, "Darling, I don't want to die in the Philippines."

I was very sad to hear that and I knew Ven did not want us to spend more money because we did not have it. He asked me to email his son Otis in the UK and ask for financial help. I also went to one of our neighbours, who was lending money as a business at 15% interest. I did not have a choice because I needed to buy the prescriptions, including the daily injections to keep Ven's blood pressure down. The following week, he improved and was arguing with the doctors again. He wanted to come out of the hospital and reluctantly they signed the papers saying it was the patient's desire to go home. Whatever happened to him now, it was not the doctors' responsibility. When preparing to check out from the hospital, I was shocked to receive a huge hospital bill of nearly 100,000 pesos, approximately £2,000 at that time, on top of all the medicine we needed to buy!

I did not know what to do, except to ask Otis for his help again, and I found another lending company and borrowed the rest of the money.

Ven was alright for a couple of months, and we went to see the goats a few weeks after he came out of hospital. We caught the bus and asked my nephew Bryan to come with us. I needed a man with me to assist Ven because he was walking with a stick now. It was a special day for us. When we arrived at the goat house, I saw the emptiness in Ven's eyes and he looked sad. He was looking at the goats for hours as he used to, but I saw the tiredness in his eyes. He was not the same Ven anymore; since he came out the hospital, he was a different person. I felt very hurt, sad and lonely.

I had shared everything with him and gained many good ideas from him about to what to do in certain situations. Although I talked to Nellie and Jennelisa, there were certain things they would not understand. I prayed to God every day that He would heal Ven from this illness. But by this time, Ven was not able to do things on his own, such as changing his clothes and having a bath. I helped him with all those things when JJ was not around.

Now I simply bought the goat feed whenever I could afford it and I left my nephew Randy to supervise the running of the minibus; he was a great help to me. I could not leave Ven on his own and I started to study alternative medicine for blood pressure and found a herbal drink. We did not have money to buy all of Ven's medicine, though I bought the main ones for his blood pressure. I also tested an alternative medicine and Ven improved tremendously after a few months of taking these. He started to talk a bit more, which I was very glad to hear.

But he said he wanted to go home and he talked about his granny and his mother, both of whom had died a long time ago. I was confused and wondered if he meant home to England or Jamaica. When I look back now, I realise he meant home to be with the Lord, because he did not want us to keep on spending money he knew we did not have.

Much of the time, he suffered headaches and screamed in pain. They kept him awake and I did not know what to do to help him. I had a hard time paying for Ven's medicine, the goats and JJ's school fees. I went to many meetings about herbal medicine

Chapter 11 - The Philippines; health and financial crises

and I decided to continue buying the ones that helped Ven. I also started to sell them to earn money. My mind was open to any alternative cures and natural medicines to avoid more huge hospital bills.

Once Ven's health was stable, my constant worry was where to get the money to maintain Ven's medication. The man who sold me the herbal teas told me that someone was working somewhere to torture Ven until he died. He said the month was already set when it was going to happen. I was very scared because he had predicted several other things in my neighbourhood that had happened to other people. I was ready to do anything as long as I could keep my husband alive. We bought Ven a gallon of herbal drink every week that was known to keep the blood pressure down. I had noticed improvements with Ven and I continued to buy him this drink. I asked the supplier what he could do to stop this witchcraft against Ven and he gave me instructions about what to do to protect my husband. I now believed that Ven's illness was not normal, and although I told no one else about what I was doing, I began to notice that Ven was getting well again.

My nephew was running the minibus business well. He came to us every evening to give us the money they had earned that day. I did not have to worry about it because he took charge of everything and I felt blessed with this nephew.

Ven and I also enjoyed a few journeys to visit the goats. We were very blessed to have Roberto looking after the goats for us. Ven's health was steady for a few months and I was very happy we could still travel on the bus to see the goats. We also asked Ross to drive the motorela up there and we did many journeys to and from the goat house. I realised I had to stop talking to Ven about any problems we had and I needed to sort them out for myself now because I did not want him to worry. I did not want to talk about my problems with my family either, because it was all about health and finance and they were unable to help me.

However, I spoke to Roger about certain things, and he asked me a few serious questions in preparation for whatever might happen to Ven. My mind was not thinking in that direction because I was not a practical person. I was simply determined to see Ven's victory from that illness and, for more than five months, Ven's health improved.

However, in July 2010, he started to have terrible headaches again. He could not get any sleep at night and we cried together and I prayed and prayed. I went to the priest to ask him again to help me to pray for Ven. I was told to light a candle for seven Fridays in the church and pray. I was also told to write the names of seven of Ven's family who were already dead, as well as give an offering of money in an envelope. I did this every Friday and for hours I was on my knees praying to God to help Ven to be healed from his illness. It was torture for me to see him rolling around the bed screaming because of the terrible headaches. I also talked to my herbal tea supplier about it and he told me that the people who are causing this were using a doll and at a certain times in the night they pierced the doll's head and every time they did it, Ven would feel the pain. I was desperate and annoyed!

I asked him, "What are you doing about it at your end?"

He simply asked for more money to buy the materials he needed to prepare something special for Ven. He said it was a two-week process and somehow I found a way to give him the money. All the time, Ven was saying that he wanted to go home and every day and I heard him calling for his deceased Mummy and Granny.

The herbal tea supplier told me many things about how these enemies operate. People who are jealous or angry with someone spend money on witchcraft to torture and destroy the victim. He said these people go to a cemetery and call on a spirit to work for them, by asking the spirit to go into the person's body. It is a very evil practice but he said it had worked with his family, from his grandparents down to his children. He said their fights with these people were always strong and sometimes it had caused deaths. However, his family felt in their hearts they were called to fight and to heal the victims, and most of the time they succeeded. He told me to do my best not to let Ven sleep at 12am and 12pm, to stop the bad spirit doing what it wanted. I did what he said and talked to Ven until after 12am and it seemed to work.

One day, I received a text from our previous healer who lived far away. He said he was coming to do a service in another city three hours' drive from us and asked me to take Ven there so he could lay hands on him and pray. We went, and after laying hands on Ven, he called me aside and said Ven's mother and granny's spirits were there visiting him, and this was destroying his health even more. It connected in my mind with what Ven had been doing when he called out for his granny and mother. He also kept saying he wanted to go home and he walked outside the house saying he wanted to go to the jackfruit tree. Melchor, Nellie's husband, always followed him. The healer told me to sacrifice chickens to these spirits to stop tormenting him.

Again, I had to find the money to do these things and we took Ven to the healer's house very early in the morning and stayed there overnight. I gave him more than 4,000 pesos, a few hundred pounds, but I believed he could help Ven because he claimed to be a new creation with the spirit of one of our famous dead heroes living in him. He said he could go to places and be invisible if he wanted to. He was more than 70 years old but he looked more like 50. He said he had healed many sick people and he could read peoples' minds.

When I told him we raised goats, he asked to have one of our breeders and we agreed to give him one.

To help Ven, he killed three big white chickens, cooked rice and placed them on the table with lots of drinks. He lit candles, prayed, and talked to Ven's mother and granny's spirits. He spoke in different languages that I did not understand. He took a very long rope and asked his son to tie the rope in front of the house and he prayed while doing it. He asked the spirits to leave Ven alone and not to disturb him again. We finished late in the afternoon and we went home.

Ven was alright after that for some months and I had to keep the businesses running and make the serious decisions on my own. I had to find the money to overhaul Ross's motorela and, at the same time, I also had to find the money for the goat's feed and the rent for where we parked our minibus and motorela. My challenge with our public transport business was that whenever I processed the renewal of the franchise, I needed to spend a lot of time to meet the requirements and I also had to spend more money. I had to make several journeys to and from offices where we needed officials to approve our vehicles. My experience in dealing with these things was not easy; some operators would pay someone to do the journeys for them and they wouldn't have to do it all themselves, but I did not have the money to pay someone else and I had to do it myself. When we started our public transport business, we had paid someone to do it for us and it was less stressful.

Then my nephew Randy decided to leave his job as a conductor on our minibus to go to Manila to find a better job. This was a big challenge for me. I was not happy about his decision because I could not think of anyone else I could trust with the minibus operation. Randy knew my struggle and he was concerned about leaving, but I did not want to stop him because I could see how much he wanted to change his situation. I hired our driver's nephew to work with him, and this worked well and meant I could be with Ven at home because he could not be left alone anymore.

One evening, I received a message that my brother Jorge had an accident while driving. I called Ross to go and find him. Fortunately, he was not hurt but he did damage the other motorela and had one passenger, who was taken to hospital, which, of course, cost me more money. Jorge's driving license was taken away by the police and he would not be able to drive again unless he paid to reclaim his license. At the time, I couldn't find a trustworthy driver for our motorela and I decided to sell it. It took us more than a month to find a buyer and I had to take a ridiculous low price. Before I could sell it, I had to pay for the loan we had taken on it. But as a result, I managed to pay some of the arrears on the bank loan, which was a huge amount of money.

Ven started to have the terrible headaches again. He could not sleep and he screamed and did not want me to leave the room, not for a minute. He wanted me to be with him all the time. I rubbed his head, and cried to the Lord for help and eventually Ven fell asleep. The next day, I asked my niece KC to watch her uncle for me while I went to find the healer again and asked what he could do about Ven's terrible headaches. He said we should do another ritual and I would need to buy materials again, but I left because I felt these things were becoming a waste of our time and money. I had lost my trust in him.

You raise me up by Leila Wilks

Ven and myself in Camiguin, White Island

Ven and I outside our home, 2008

Chapter 12 - The Philippines; healers, helpers and hospitals

One night, Ven was struggling to breathe, so I called my nephew Ronillo and asked him to help me to take Ven to the hospital. We took him to the same private hospital we had been to before because we already knew the doctors there. I did not think about money this time; I simply wanted the best treatment for Ven.

Three days later, they decided to send Ven for dialysis. My niece lent me a couple of thousand pesos. I had to go home and sort out the things we needed in the hospital. The doctor told me Ven had to stay in the hospital because if he went home too soon, he would die. He was required to go on dialysis once a week, and I was grateful to Ronillo who was able to be there to help me. I needed a man to lift Ven up and I needed someone to stay with him while I went round to find the money to buy his prescriptions.

I also had JJ's school requirements to finance. I went to places I had never been before and meet people I had never before approached about money to keep Ven in the hospital. Ven's money from England was not enough, so I started to contact more people we knew in England because I had run out of people to go to in the Philippines. I contacted Ven's cousin, nephew, brother and sister. I told them about Ven's health condition and our financial needs. However, they all had their own problems and could not help. I went through Ven's friends' contact numbers in his diary but none of them were able to help either. It was a daily headache for me to find money to buy his medicines. I cried and cried and felt really hopeless. I felt very empty and lost. JJ slept in the hospital every weekend and visited his dad every evening after school, coming home at 11pm with his cousins, Rhyme, SeanJohn and Justin. My family did everything they could to help and support me, but my biggest need was for finance, and that was a struggle for everyone. I made a list of people I could contact. One of them was my father's sister. I never thought of contacting her before. She was not happy with me when I went to England and I did not communicate with her. But by this time, I had run out of people to call on for help, so I sent a message to Aunt Adelfa. She asked me to come and see her and she lent me a couple of thousand pesos.

Ven was not a happy person any more. He did not want to see people and he did not want to communicate to anyone. I felt very hurt and sad about it on top of what I was going through. Every time he talked, it was always about wanting to go home. It was very painful to see him in this state, knowing what he had been like before the illness. He had been such a very happy man!

However, I was relieved that our minibus business, now being managed by someone, was doing well and earning money every day for us. It was not a great amount, but it was a real help.

My life was focused on our debts. Whenever we had a little more money, I reduced our loans. By this time, Ven was in a bad condition. We had to wipe him, feed him and turn him from side to side because he could not move himself anymore. Looking at Ven's situation, everything I was trying seemed hopeless. I knew I did not have sufficient income to keep on buying all the medicine he needed, and I had already run out of people who could lend us more money. I did not know what to do. Suddenly I remembered my friend Glory Tan, who used to work with us in our first business. Since we had stopped working on that business, I hadn't communicated with her. I knew she was a Christian and I felt I needed to send her a message about Ven's health. She came to the hospital and was shocked to see Ven's condition, but she promised to come back the next day with a pastor to pray for Ven. I was very glad to hear this, and when they arrived, we all prayed together. The next day, Ven started to talk. The doctor sent him for many tests and arranged for him to have a tube in his nostril for his liquid food. He continued on dialysis. It was a struggle every day to buy the doctor's prescriptions to keep his blood pressure down and his heart under control. Every time they handed me a prescription, I did not even have enough time to think where to get the money from to buy it. It was needed at a specific hour every day and cost thousands and thousands, as well as the hospital bill; the daily charge of that was very high. Sometimes we had to take Ven to different hospitals for other treatments, and that was an additional cost.

I was in regular contact with Roger and Paula, and they kept telling me to come back to England because the situation we were in was overwhelming. However, I kept thinking that because we had nothing in England, how would we manage if we did go back? There were also the goats, the pigs and JJ's schooling to consider, and we did not have the money for the journey back. Roger kept warning me to get ready emotionally for whatever might happen to Ven in the days ahead. I felt very lost and could not think straight. What I was focusing on was doing everything I could to keep Ven alive and somehow find enough money to buy his medicine and take him out of the hospital. Ven seemed to be improving but he was now in a wheelchair. He had been in a private hospital for three weeks and our hospital bill was more than 78,000 pesos.

I did not have much left from the money I gained by pawning our vehicles because I had used it to pay off our other loans. I rang Roger and he sent me the money I needed to check Ven out of the hospital. After the hospitalisation, we went to City Alliance Church where Glory introduced us to Pastor Noel Treveligio, who ran the church together with his wife, Cecille. We were made very welcome and they prayed for us on a regular basis. Ven started crying when he heard the word of God and so did I. At last, we had found a church that would listen to us, support and encourage us to carry on; it felt as though it was meant to happen. When I had thought about Glory in the hospital, I felt an urgency to get back to her as a friend and be connected with other good friends. And as it happened, our first experience in the church was very dramatic. The pastor's message seemed to be directly talking about us and about God's plan for us. *"When the student is ready, the teacher will appear,"* and so it was!

I remember Ven and I were sobbing as we listened to the message, and Ven said, "Yes!"

Ven's parents had been Christians, and when he was growing up, he heard the words of God regularly, and these words comforted him now in his illness.

After the church service, Pastor Noel told me he remembered seeing Ven at Glory's wedding anniversary party. At that time, he was a very happy man, dancing and singing at the party. I remembered that particular occasion too, and I told Pastor Noel briefly about what had been happening to us. He asked me to come and see him in his office the next day to tell him the whole story.

The next morning, I asked Ronillo to look after his uncle for me, and I went and told the Pastor everything since we had noticed the changes in our lives. Pastor Noel arranged for Pastor Val to go and do a Bible study for us once a week. From then on, we went to church every Sunday as a family. I cried most of the time hearing the word of God. It felt as though I had been starved! The more I heard the words, the more I wanted to hear. Pastor Noel also encouraged me to read the Bible every day. They even gave JJ and I Bibles, which made me happy, and I started to read it as much as I could. His wife came to do the Bible study with him, and Ven was always willing to participate; Pastor Val and Elie prayed with him. Sadly, Ven had changed completely and was not the same person he used to be. Now he looked down on the floor and was blank.

Chapter 12 - The Philippines; healers, helpers and hospitals

During September 2010, Ven struggled to breathe again and had terrible headaches. He cried out, saying, "I am not going to die here, I want to go home."

We rushed him to the same private hospital again and, once there, Ven had another stroke. This was the third one he had suffered. The doctor said he had to go on dialysis three times a week, but we could not afford it, so the doctor said at least twice a week. His medicine was increased to fifteen tablets a day and he had to stay in the hospital for three weeks again. Once more, I had a big challenge to find the money to pay the hospital bill. My friend Glory and her husband Roly came to the hospital and gave us financial support, and I was so very grateful.

I went to the hospital director and asked if I could make a promise to pay the rest by instalments so they could release my husband. I stood in front of him begging for his approval, but he was not compassionate and simply told me that if he would allow us to pay the rest of the bill in that way, he would have to do it for all the other people. Obviously, he was not interested in helping us, so I had to find another way for Ven to go home to avoid paying more daily room charges in the hospital. I asked one of my nieces if she could help me with the rest of the bill and she applied for a bank loan using her land title as collateral. She made me promise to pay her back in six months' time because she did not want her husband to know about it. I went through many struggles to pay that money back to her, but I did it.

Every day, Ven was in the hospital, I had to go home to sort out JJ's school requirements, food and pay the bills. The hospital became our second home, and I asked my niece KC to stay in the house so there was someone at home for JJ. After we paid the final hospital bill, we were able to take Ven home, although we had to take him to another private clinic for regular check-ups. Once we were home, Glory came to visit us several times and brought us food, fruit and food supplements for Ven.

The next drama was that our home was soon to be foreclosed because we could not pay the bank loan we had secured against it as collateral. Now everything seemed upside down. I had payments to make, weekly and monthly, for the vehicle loans and the money I had borrowed from different lending companies at very high interest rates. I had many people chasing me for their money. Ven was required to go on dialysis twice a week now and I had to find his blood match for blood transfusions, pay for the dialysis service, plus the doctor's charge. The dialysis cost 3,500 pesos, not including the blood, and we had to cover our public transport to the hospital.

Ven also needed to be in a wheelchair, which I had to buy. Before we found a cheap second-hand one, JJ and Ronillo carried Ven on their backs to the main road because there was no vehicle that could come to the front of the house. I was doing everything I could to find the money twice a week. I had to stop buying the herbal tea for him and I focused on buying the tablets he needed instead. We had to eat porridge most of the time to survive because we could not afford to buy fish and rice, although I always made sure Ven had rice and fish, even if JJ and I went without.

After two months of this routine, I could no longer afford his dialysis twice a week. I explained it to the doctor, but he said it was very risky to miss even one dialysis. I realised the doctor could not help me and it was up to me to work out what to do. I knew I needed to sell the goats. I went to three restaurants to negotiate the price and found one that would pay more than the others. We used our minibus to transport them but it was a very painful experience selling these animals. We had to select the healthiest ones and these, of course, included our favourites, Barako, our breeder, Honey, and 54, as well as a few of the young ones too.

JJ came with us and we put Ven near the goats and I explained to him what we were doing. Even though he was very weak,

Chapter 12 - The Philippines; healers, helpers and hospitals

he slowly stroked the goats one by one. I started crying and felt very hurt by what I had to do! I had learnt to love them and they had become very special to me too. When we travelled back to our city, one of them became very sick and when we arrived at the restaurant, the goat died on Roberto's lap. Now we only had five to sell. We had to leave as soon as they paid us the money because we were all sad and trying not to cry.

The next day, we took Ven to dialysis. However, that week we missed one dialysis session, and three days later, Ven was struggling to breathe. We had to rush him to the hospital again. For the very first time, we had to take him to a public hospital because I could not afford to take him back to a private hospital anymore. We did not have money even to pay for a taxi; I had to call our driver Ross to take us there. We had to wait a long time before Ven could get treatment. The whole night we were in the emergency room with folding beds lined up. We saw many people around us who were dying. I talked to the doctor and nurses, pleading them to get my husband's treatment, but it did not make any difference because there were many patients ahead of us.

However, I was very anxious because Ven was struggling to breathe, and I approached a doctor and begged him to attend to Ven next. When he looked at Ven, he saw he was a foreigner and he went straight to him. He asked the nurse to check Ven's blood pressure while he was interviewing me. The doctor gave Ven medication and we were put in a queue to be admitted. It was a really long queue because they had run out of patient rooms. We waited a whole day to be admitted. I rang my friend Helen and told her about our situation in the hospital. Helen and Steve were friends with a couple of German doctors and it was called the German Doctors' Hospital. It was not a big hospital and they only treated a small amount of patients, but they supplied medicine to people who could not afford to pay.

You raise me up by Leila Wilks

In the hospital, it was a struggle because Ven did not want to stay there. He was fighting with us and saying he wanted to go home. We had to hold him and he often pulled out the drip needle from his arm and the food tube from his nostrils. This did not help to reduce his blood pressure and I had to ask one of my nephews to be there to help me with him all the time. These were torturing moments for me as I watched my husband in that condition. I knew he was not comfortable with all those tubes connected to his body.

I went home that day leaving my nephew to watch Ven. My sister Nellie was there as well. At home, while I was preparing things for JJ's school projects and lunch, I poured out my emotions, crying and crying! While smoking again, I realised how I was in a catch-22 situation because if I didn't take Ven to dialysis twice a week as required, he would be admitted to the hospital and there would be more expense. Either way, it was difficult for me because Ven's pension money was not enough for what we needed to pay.

Once, when Ven was in the hospital for four days, we had a hospital bill of 18,000 pesos, not including the daily medical expenses. Before Ven came out of the hospital, Pastor Noel went there while I was at home, and prayed for Ven. He also gave us money that day, which helped to buy food and Ven's medicine. I managed to borrow another 10,000 from one of our neighbours, who charged 15% interest, and I went around the neighbourhood looking for more loans to cover the 8,000 or so we still owed. One lady lent me 5,000, and for the last 3,000, I went to my niece again and made a promise to pay her back with 10% interest in one month's time. Having raised the money to pay the bill, I was allowed to take Ven home, although the doctors did not want to discharge him.

In the public hospital room, they had four patients in four beds sharing one toilet. The relatives and the patients shared the same

Chapter 12 - The Philippines; healers, helpers and hospitals

toilets and it was disgustingly dirty most of the time. We did not get a proper sleep at night because there was nowhere to put our heads down. I had to put my head on the edge of Ven's single bed. I asked the family to help me to be there in turn. They provided one chair for each patient. I sat there overnight and held Ven's hand so if I nodded off when he was trying to get up, I would wake up. Doing this on my own was very hard. Ven kept on calling for me because he didn't feel comfortable if he couldn't see me.

We had to sign another paper again before we took Ven out of the hospital, saying that whatever happened to the patient was not the doctor's responsibility because the patient chose to go home. This time I decided I had to do everything I could to take Ven to dialysis twice a week to avoid being admitted to hospital again. I went through everything I could think of to have enough money to pay for the treatment. I wrote down what I could sell and where I could get more loans. On Sunday nights, I refused to go to bed until I knew what I had to do the next day to raise money for Ven. The dialysis cost 7,000 pesos a week, plus the blood and the tablets. I remembered to focus on the solution of each problem and kept a written record of what I was doing. I borrowed more money to pay off the person who was charging the highest interest, and I fulfilled my promise and settled up with my niece.

You raise me up by Leila Wilks

My cousin Elisa, Nellie, myself, JJ, Uncle Democrito and his wife Aunty Estelita in 2015

Aunty Adelfa and myself

Chapter 13 - The Philippines; hope shines bright in the darkness

Out of the blue, another challenge faced me. Our minibus driver was not well and I could not find an alternative driver to keep the minibus running to earn the money we so badly needed. Sadly, the minibus was parked up for two days until our driver was well again.

I was experiencing tremendous pressure to find the money to send Ven to dialysis twice a week. Ven's pension money that came every month was now going straight to the people I had borrowed from, and often it was not even enough to pay them. All the money I borrowed had interest to pay as well, sometimes 10% and sometimes as high as 18% interest. It encouraged people in my area to lend me the money because all of them knew I needed it every week for the dialysis. I also had bank loans every month to pay, vehicle collateral loans and small lending companies loans. I was in this over my head and did not know what to do. I felt as if I was being buried alive.

Even though we were in this struggle, we managed to go to church every Sunday as a family. JJ put his dad in a wheelchair and pushed him to the main road where we hired a motorela because we needed the space for the wheelchair. It was an extra expense, but I knew we needed to hear God's Word. We loved the Sunday service and the people in the church were so welcoming. Hearing the Word of God gave us all encouragement, strength, guidance and, for me, the courage to carry on. We also made many friends in the church and Pastor Val came to our home every week to do Bible study. Ven said to him, "Pastor, I am going home."

It hurt me because I thought he wanted to go home to England and I could not see how it could happen because we did not have a home in England anymore. Also, when I talked to Roger on the phone, he always said, "Come home to England."

The practical thing to do was to return to England, but I did not know how we could in our position. We still had JJ at school, the minibus business and the remaining goats. However, a few months after running the minibus, Ronillo decided to stop. Roberto's son offered to help and I had to trust him to keep the minibus running, collect the money, pay the driver, take his commission and give me the rest. I continued to struggle every day, looking after Ven and looking for a way to pay JJ's monthly tuition on top of everything else. I was also running the home and paying off the money I owed to different people. The bank manager was contacting me on a regular basis because I was behind with my bank loan payments. I went to see her and cried a few times when I explained about my struggles, but as we all knew, they were simply doing their job. She told me they would take the house from us if I did not pay a certain amount that month. I went home that day and cried in the bedroom; Ven held me, trying to calm me down. I could not feel any energy from him, although he was trying to reassure me without words. I cried even more, because it hurt me to see him like that. I missed how we used to solve problems together, talking about them and focusing on solutions, not dwelling on the problems.

But now, seeing Ven like that was torture for me because I realised I was on my own facing these struggles.

I cried out loud, "Lord, why did you allow these things to happen to him and to us? Where are you?"

I kept my emotional and financial struggles hidden from JJ. I did not want him to know how bad our problems were; I did not want him to worry. Every time JJ needed to attend an exam and I needed to pay for his tuition, I had to join a long queue and make a promise about when to pay the money, even though

Chapter 13 - The Philippines; hope shines bright in the darkness

I did not know where to find this money. The next day, I went everywhere to find the money because the school only gave us a short time and if we didn't deliver, JJ would be refused school exams. Most of the people in my neighbourhood did not run lending businesses, but they lent me the money because there was interest on it.

A few days after paying JJ's tuition, I received a final demand notice for our electricity connection because I had not paid that bill. I had to find another neighbour to borrow money from to pay that too. It was not a good way to live!

I also asked people about alternative remedies for high blood pressure. I learnt that guanabana* leaves and lemon grass boiled are good for reducing blood pressure. I attended a meeting and bought these extract products, which were not cheap! I boiled lemon grass and guanabana leaves on a regular basis and gave it to Ven to drink. After a few months, Ven started to feel more energy and his blood pressure was controlled. The products were not cheap, but it was much better than the tablets and we saw a real improvement, although I still bought the necessary tablets for him.

I tried sending messages to Ven's family in England and Jamaica, telling them about his health situation and asking for financial help again. Most of them said they did not have the money to help. I can understand why people are reluctant to help someone abroad. They think they are being used and they do not know the person well enough to realise they would never ask for money unless they were desperate. I believe if we are able to help someone who is desperate, we should do so because if they die, we won't have that opportunity anymore to help! We should be prepared to express our concern and love for people while they are still alive.

A friend of mine then offered to help and I was so happy because I had enough money to send Ven to dialysis again. He hated going and every time we took him there, he was annoyed and it was a challenge to get him ready. We talked to Pastor Noel and Val about our experiences, and they suggested we removed all the witchcraft protection products in the house. I saw the sense in doing this now, although I had never before relied on God to deal with my struggles. However, I took their advice and gathered up all the stuff and I took it with us to church one Sunday. After the service, Pastor Noel and helpers from the church burnt these items behind the church, and I felt cleansed by the experience.

We continued to do Bible study with Pastor Val and Elie, and they became very close to us. Now I felt free to tell Pastor Noel everything that was happening and I gave him an update about Ven's situation. He was a very warm and caring person, and I was comfortable talking to him about my challenges. He always gave me financial support. He told me to see the secretary, Sister Norma, to collect the money for Ven's dialysis. He also knew someone in authority in the hospital who helped us get free blood for Ven. It was a great help.

As we approached Christmas 2010, Ven had improved with his herbal medicine, boiled leaves and his maintenance tablets on top of the twice a week dialysis. Pastor Noel recommended I read the Psalms to Ven every night; he liked to hear the words and always said, "Amen." I also played the CD of *Stand Up For Jesus* by Jackie Edward and left it playing in the background while Ven was going to sleep.

On New Year's Day 2011, JJ went out with his cousins, while Ven and I were at home. I looked at Ven sleeping, and although I was not sure what would happen to us, I felt I was getting stronger. I started to see a hope of Ven getting better from his illness. This was a new year that would give us a way out of this situation. My positive mind started to work again. I started praying for

Chapter 13 - The Philippines; hope shines bright in the darkness

Ven's full recovery. I did not mind losing every material thing we possessed, as long as his health returned. I had a strong belief things would change for the better. I started making plans about what to do every day, who to see about money, so Ven could be on dialysis on a regular basis. The more I thought about it, the more fresh ideas came to my mind. Hope shone bright in the darkness that evening.

We had a piece of land in Alicomohan that we had bought where we used to have our little house on top of the hill, overlooking the sea and the main road. The land had been owned by one of Papa's sisters and it had sentimental value for me because it was where we had run away to as children when the Marcos government rebels attacked the villages. We had terrible family arguments over this land and who actually owned it, but in the end, we did, and I decided that now was the time to sell it. I found a buyer and it was a great help for Ven's dialysis and medicines, and I was also able to pay off several of our outstanding loans. The price we sold it for was ridiculous, but at that time any amount of money was useful. I did not think about what I had lost; my priority was saving Ven's life. After paying the debts, I had a mere 15,000 pesos in my hand, but that was something!

Around this time, JJ was heading towards his last exam and graduation in high school. It was very hard for me because I was one month behind with the school payment and he had to prepare for his graduation. I did not have enough money to pay for his final tuition. The school principal would not allow JJ to take the final exams unless I paid the money I owed the school. I cried and told him I was having a very hard time and explained about Ven's illness. I told him that all our money went towards my husband's dialysis and medication because we wanted him to live. He was quiet, but he reached for the pen and he signed a promissory paper allowing JJ to take his final exams and graduate.

135

Next, I went to the electricity company and water supplier because we'd had another final demand notice from them both to cut our connection if we did not pay their bills. After explaining our situation again, I was given extension days. From there, I went to different places to look for more herbal drinks for Ven.

On JJ's graduation day, he was very sad his dad could not be there. I was very happy inside despite what we had gone through. I had managed to finance JJ's education until he finished. But also at the bottom of my heart, I too was very sad because Ven could not join us. Although I did not have much money, we celebrated JJ's graduation day. We bought roasted chicken and ate it with rice with JJ's cousins at our home.

After JJ's graduation day, I was not sure where our lives were heading. Ven and I had always wanted him to do something great with his life. We had talked about how we would support and help him in what he wanted to build for his future. What hurt me so much was when we came home from JJ's graduation, Ven did not know what was happening. No matter how much I talked to him and explained things, he just nodded his head as a sign that he had heard me, but he had become very quiet since the third stroke. When I prayed for him, I told him how exciting it would be when he recovered from this illness. I reminded him of what we used to say to each other.

"It's never over until it's over and we will never give up in life. We will live life as long as there is life to live."

I reminded him that he was tough and he had been through a lot in life, but he had always come out victorious. Every time I talked to him about these things, I had to work hard to hold on to my tears; I did not want him to see me cry, and when I felt I could no longer stop myself from crying, I went into the toilet and let go and burst out crying there. I did not talk to anyone about how troubled I was inside my heart. I felt fearful because I could see

Chapter 13 - The Philippines; hope shines bright in the darkness

Ven's illness was not getting better, I could see that we could lose him at any time. I was tortured and very scared every day.

Pastor Val and Elie continued to come to our home to conduct Bible study with us. I was desperate for us to be baptised but they insisted that we needed to learn more about the Word of God.

Eventually, Pastor Noel arranged a date for us to be baptised at the beach, and on April 18th 2011, Ven, JJ and I were baptised.
 I remember Pastor Noel said to me that day that when we go back to England, I should find a church which strongly preaches the Word of God, and he gave me the names of a few denominations.

You raise me up by Leila Wilks

Chapter 14 - The Philippines; debts, dialysis and more disasters

In April, it was JJ's birthday. I wanted us to go to the beach with the family and enjoy roasted fish and nice drinks. Ven's health was stable because he was getting regular dialysis treatment and I was able to buy his tablets.

During Easter week, I felt I needed to take JJ to the place where I grew up, in the mountain of Kalakaran, Manoligao in Carmen. It is a five-hour ride from our city in Cagayan, but I wanted JJ to see the place, and meet the lady who hid me in their bedroom when my father was looking for me and wanted to kill me when I was only 14 years old. My sister Nellie, her husband Melchor, their children, my sister Jennelisa and her daughter Kate came with us. I left Ven with my nephew Ronillo.

We stayed one night in Carmen, and early the next morning, we hired three big motorbikes to climb up to the mountain of Manoligao and we walked to Kalakaran because no vehicles can go there. We went up there with Sammy, one of my cousins who I had grown up with in the same area. All of us walked across the seven rivers to reach our destination and I showed JJ the river where I was nearly drowned, and we passed the place where we used to live as a family on the farm. The place was empty with old coconut trees around it. We went to one of our cousin's house nearby and had lunch with them and the family. We showed JJ my father's old farm and the river where we bathed, washed our clothes and caught prawns. We filmed and took photos of it all. I am not sure if we would ever go back there again, but I was happy that JJ had seen these things and had understood how hard our lives had been in my childhood and my stories had come alive for him.

After this happy excursion, there were more challenges ahead for me to deal with. One day, our driver bumped into a policeman and had to transfer his passengers to another bus and refund all their fares because the police held him in the police station with our minibus. I had to bail him out, which cost me a lot of money and it took me three days to sort out. I managed to borrow money again from a small lending company. We relied on our minibus to earn us money every day, and because of this unexpected event, I could not buy Ven's regular medicine that month.

A week after that incident, our driver said there was something wrong with the bus that he could not fix himself. We had to take it to the repair shop and discovered it needed overhauling. This was another very stressful experience for me to deal with. It would cost us a lot of money to do the overhaul work, but if I didn't have it done, we would not have an income for our daily needs. Although Ross was still driving our motorela, it did not provide a sufficient income. I also had a regular payment to make to the lending companies where I still owed money and where I had the motorela and the bus as collateral. There was also a bank loan to pay. I had to go everywhere to find the money.

Roger and Paula came to my mind. I did not have any hope about finding the money locally when I explained to Roger what had happened and what we needed to do. I told Roger that the minibus was our only hope to earn the money we needed to buy Ven's medicine. Roger was very compassionate, as always, and he sent me the £500 for the minibus overhaul.

Then, early one morning, Ven was struggling to breathe again, so I woke up JJ and my niece KC and sister Nellie to help me to get transport to take Ven to the hospital. JJ and I put Ven in his wheelchair and rushed him to the main road. It was a very worrying moment because we were taking him to the public hospital again. I talked to the doctor, begged him to help my

Chapter 14 - The Philippines; debts, dialysis and more disasters

husband. This was in the emergency department, a place that was always full and most patients had serious sickness that all needed urgent treatment. It was fortunate that the doctor attended to Ven straight away and his breathing was stabilised. It was always the case; every time Ven missed one dialysis session, he struggled to breathe. He had missed one when the minibus was not running. It was a catch-22 situation because we already had an outstanding bill at the hospital from a previous dialysis, as most of the time, I could not pay the full amount. I had to go to the head of the hospital and take a note for him to sign so Ven could have his dialysis. It was a struggle every time I went there because most of the time, this person was not there and we had to wait for a long time, and the assistant staff were not helpful. A few times, I was told to come back the next day! I was desperate for Ven to have his dialysis. Sometimes I cried in front of this assistant, saying, "I do not want my husband to die, please help me to get this note signed. He needs his dialysis done now!"

Every time Ven had his dialysis, the bills added up because I could not get enough money to cover it and it was a lot of money every time. We had to buy a bag of blood before we could start the treatment. I'd heard about someone selling blood in the hospital and I had to negotiate with this person, but I did get what Ven needed far cheaper than the hospital blood supply. This time, Ven was in the hospital for a week; in fact, the doctor did not want to send him home, but as usual Ven did everything with his small amount of energy to get up and walk out of the door, if we did not keep our eyes on him. We had to watch him all the time. He did not want to listen to anyone, except me. He calmed down when I was with him, but I had to go everywhere to find money to buy his prescription and, at the same time, check the minibus situation. When I felt I could not go on any more, I went home and I cried inside our bathroom as much as I could. I stayed in the toilet and smoked for hours. Then I heard the song, *You Raise Me Up** being sung by Josh Groban on the radio next door. I heard it lots of times and it encouraged me to carry on.

You raise me up by Leila Wilks

> *"You raise me up, so I can stand on mountains.*
> *You raise me up to walk in stormy seas.*
> *I am strong when I am on your shoulders.*
> *You raise me up to more than I can be."*

The next morning while walking around the hospital, I noticed a very long queue. I asked what they were queuing for. The lady told me they were going to ask for help from the head of the political party so they could have a reduction from their dialysis and hospital bills. She told me we had to vote for this party. I did not care who I voted for, as long as I could get help for Ven's dialysis bill.

However, it was not enough and, in the end, I decide to sell the moterela. I owed money for it from the lending company as collateral and I had to pay that money back first and hardly had any money left after the sale. Now we only had the minibus running to provide an income. However, on May 18th 2011, an even worse disaster struck our lives, and our minibus had a fatal accident; three people died. My mind went blank! I did not know what to do. I knew it was up to me to act, and the morning after the accident, as soon as the sun was shining and the neighbours were up, I went around the area to find out who could lend me money to visit the victims and sort out the minibus. I asked JJ to look after his dad. I had to go to the hospital first and then the police station. When I passed the area where the accident happened, I saw our minibus. It was really smashed up. I was crying inside the bus I was travelling on as we passed the wreckage. I felt such pain looking at the only thing we had left to earn an income to put food on the table and buy Ven's medicine and go towards his dialysis costs. I thought it was a terrible nightmare! I was hoping it was...

The reality came home to me when I reached the hospital and was handed the records of the dead victims of the accident, including: our bus driver; a soldier sitting next to the driver; and a

Chapter 14 - The Philippines; debts, dialysis and more disasters

lady, sitting behind the driver. They had died instantly in our bus, when they had a head-on collision with a big logging truck. The dead bodies were taken to the funeral homes and later on their families came to take them home to bury them. I had to pay for all their funeral bills and the hospital bills from my own pocket because the insurance had to be processed and it would take a long time. I went to the police station and met up with the driver of the logging truck and sorted out the details with the police. It was a very unpleasant experience, especially on my own.

At the same time, I had to think about Ven; I was concerned about how he was while I was away from home. I was constantly texting with my niece KC and JJ. Nellie and her husband Melchor sent me a message that I should not worry about Ven because they would look after him on my behalf. I should focus on what I needed to do. I was told by the insurance company it would take a month before they could pay me because they would process the papers in Manila. I was very irritated! I argued with the person who was dealing with it. I explained why I needed to get it as quickly as possible because of my family situation, but they were unable to help me. There was so much hassle, witnesses to talk with and paperwork to deal with, and it was taking so much of my time that I could hardly go around to find the money for Ven's next dialysis. I felt numb. I did not have time to stop and think! I had to cope with all the expenses and I had to keep going back to be interviewed by the police and to deal with all the demands from the families of the victims. It was three hours from home by bus. I cried in front of the police officers and told them about my husband's serious health situation, but there was little they could do to help me.

It was my responsibility. I cried everywhere I went. I did not know who to ask for help. It reminded me of my struggle and pain when I had lost my mother. I was constantly borrowing money from everywhere I could and it broke my heart to see our minibus smashed up every time I went past it on the road.

143

You raise me up by Leila Wilks

I was advised to sell the minibus to the scrap buyer, but of course, I had borrowed money from a lending company using the minibus as collateral and I had to pay them first. It was very hard emotionally, mentally and physically. The lending company was following me as if I was a criminal, and I was on the go all the time, with all these people on my back wanting money from me: the victims; the hospital; the police; the witnesses; and the lending companies.

On the day I signed the sales papers, we had to trailer the minibus to the scrap merchant and it broke my heart doing this. I said goodbye to Super Red for the last time and I was really suffering inside my heart. The minibus had been a good runner and had served us well and earned us good, honest money, but the lending company manager simply grinned at me and he had no idea how painful that day was for me. It is such a very unhappy memory, and in such sad circumstances. By the time I sold our trusty minibus for scrap, I was left on my own, with only a few hundred pesos in my hand. At that moment, I was very lost and helpless, I did not know where to go. I felt completely crushed. I did not know where to get money from for Ven's next dialysis. I felt led to see Pastor Noel. I went to his office, but could not say a word. I burst out crying. Afterwards, when I had told him everything, he prayed for me.

That week at our Sunday church service, all the church family prayed over us and gave us the offering they had collected on that day. Pastor Noel placed it in the envelope and gave it to us. I cried! I felt loved and reassured that this too will come to pass and things will get better.

However, the victim's families kept coming to see me asking for help and for more money, for their hospital bills, medicine, funerals, and it broke my heart that our minibus had caused such trauma and pain for so many people. The dead driver's wife asked me for the money to finance her husband's funeral

Chapter 14 - The Philippines; debts, dialysis and more disasters

and I felt devastated for her. What a painful thing to hear a wife say that she could not afford to bury her husband. They had no money and she had many children to feed. She could not even afford to buy her husband a coffin. Then the husband of the lady who died also came and asked me to help him with his funeral costs. Their son, who had broken his leg in the accident, was transferred to our local hospital where we took Ven for dialysis. When the doctor's had to amputate his leg and replace it with a false one, I had to find more money for his treatment and his medicine. In fact, the boy's hospital bill was in my name and I was responsible for all his expenses! I had to continue following up with the insurance company and I had to collect all the dead people's details and deal with the poor grieving families. It was a terrible time for so many people. The dead soldier's wife then sued me for costs and kept demanding more and more money, which nearly finished me off!

Fortunately, during this terrible time Ven was stable, although we had missed a few of Ven's dialysis sessions because I did not have the money to pay and I had not paid the big bill from the previous ones.

I went to Uncle Isabelo and asked if he knew someone I could borrow money from. He took me to see the vet who had helped us with the goats and pigs. He had a daughter abroad who sent him money. When we got there, he asked if he could buy our remaining 22 goats and he said he would talk to his daughter abroad and ask if she would give him the money to pay me. He said he would not buy them though if we would not give him the goat house as well. I was shocked to hear this and I said no, only the goats. He said, "Well, I am not going to contact my daughter, you might as well sell them to other people."

I could not believe him! I felt like slapping his face, but I couldn't. He knew it was not easy for me to find a buyer. He was taking advantage of the opportunity to get the goats and our goat house

145

at a ridiculous price because he knew I was desperate. He had no interest in helping us. I was very crushed inside and really angry with him. I said I would go home and get back to him if I needed to. When I got home, I could not stop thinking about our goats. I had become very attached to them, but I did not have any other way to find money for Ven's dialysis. That month, Ven had missed a few treatments already. I was very scared that he would be admitted into the hospital again and I would have to spend more money. Thinking about these things made me decide to let the goats go with their goat house. This was very painful for me to do, and I knew that I was being taken advantage of, but I had no choice.

One morning, when Ven was very sick, I got scared and thought we would lose him that day. I sent an email to his son Otis in the UK. I told him to be ready because any time from now, we could lose his dad. He replied immediately asking how much the plane tickets for the three of us to go back to England would cost. As I have checked, I realised JJ's passport had expired so Otis sent me the money to renew it; I had to borrow money from Steve and Helen while waiting for the money that Otis would send so I could do it as soon as possible. Otis also gave me instructions about how to apply for housing accommodation in England. I also contacted my friend Mark, who replied that there was a holiday caravan near his home and we could use it as a temporary accommodation. The main thing was for us to go back to England, no matter what.

Then, one evening, I was struggling to breathe; I was having a bad asthma attack! All these bad and highly emotional experiences were causing my body to shut down, I believed. Now we did not have money for anything at all. My family helped me, sat me up on the bed and rubbed anything they could, and gave me herbal drinks. Fortunately, my sister Jennelisa had a nebuliser so I used it. I was still breathing hard and needed a lot of air. My nieces KC and Lea helped me by using a hand fan continuously.

Chapter 14 - The Philippines; debts, dialysis and more disasters

Early the next morning, Ven was struggling to breathe, even as I was struggling myself. I did not have time to call for help, I had to get up and sit him up and run upstairs to ask JJ to get his dad to the hospital. Everyone was up, my sister next door and her family. They took Ven to the hospital. I forgot that I was sick and went with them to the hospital and, amazingly, my asthma got better.

I left Ven in the hospital with Nellie and Jennelisa and went to find Pastor Noel. He gave me money because we did not have food in the house and we needed money now to pay for the hospital again. All the doctors there knew us and you could see it in their eyes saying, "Here they are again."

Glory visited us in the hospital, and every time she came, she always brought something for us. No one knew how much money I owed the hospital, and this time I was even more concerned about how I would pay for it. Pastor Val and Elie continued to come to our house for a Bible study every week and all the church family were constantly praying for us. I went to the prayer night a few times. I did not have a clue how powerful prayers are. They would cry with us and kept encouraging us.

I remember once, when Ven was about to come out of the hospital, I was lost as to what to do next because we did not have any money. Pastor Val came to our house without me asking and he gave me money. He took me with him to the hospital because Pastor Noel had been admitted to a private hospital. He was not well, but when he saw me, he was concerned about Ven and asked many questions. It was as if I was the one who was sick in the hospital and he was visiting me! It was all about us and at that moment he told me he would ring his secretary, Sister Norma, and tell her to give me more money. I was very touched. I did not have a chance to ask him how he was. Pastor Val talked to him and he said he was waiting for his check-up result. His illness was serious. He said to Pastor Val to take me to the church

147

to get the money straight away. The only thing that helped me to be strong was seeing them in the church regularly and hearing messages from the Bible; it placed me in the right direction.

Ven came out of the hospital again and we managed to pay some of the previous hospital bills. I was sent to the head of the hospital again and had to sign another promissory note so they could send Ven home. I still owed a huge bill from the hospital.

Our prayers were answered, however, because after that hospitalisation, Ven's health stabilised again and Glory Tan helped me regularly pay for Ven's dialysis. Ven started to get up and walk around the house. I was very happy, although he was still very quiet and never said a word. Almost every week, I was in Glory's office and shop. I felt embarrassed asking for her help so regularly, but I did not have any other way to find the money. Every time I went there, she asked her staff to put toiletries in a bag for me to take home. I also started selling things that we no longer needed from our home. This helped to finance the dialysis, together with the generous help from Glory Tan.

Chapter 15 - The Philippines; spirits, miracles, Typhoon Sendong

Ven, JJ and I continued to go to church every Sunday while waiting for JJ's passport and hearing from the housing association in England. At this stage, Otis and his ex-wife were already planning to take the three of us to live in his apartment until we got back on our feet. Otis took out a bank loan to send us the money for our plane tickets. I was getting everything in the house packed, the things we needed, and selling the rest of the appliances. Doing what I was doing had given me a hope that Ven would get better when he went back to England.

Our plan was to book our flight in January 2012. Although I was excited, I was also very worried about how we could leave the bill in the hospital. I was worried the doctor would not sign the permit to allow Ven to travel on the plane because of the advanced stage of his illness. I was also very concerned about the money I still owed other people, including the lending companies and the bank loans.

However, I got excited when JJ's passport arrived and I could feel the reality of going back to England. Then, unexpectedly, I was so sick with a horrible infection and I was in terrible pain. The doctor said I needed a small operation, but because Otis was preparing for us back in England, I emailed him and told him I needed this operation done as soon as possible. Fortunately, he sent me the money and I had the operation. I promised to pay him all of this money when we got settled in England.

By now, Ven was walking around the house and wanted to go outside. We had to watch him all the time. One morning, he got up and went straight outside the house. I was walking behind him, and I asked him, "Where are you going, darling?"

To my amazement, he spoke to me and said, "I am going home. I want to go to the jack fruit tree."

Was it home to Jamaica or England? I asked him this.

He did not answer me, but he kept walking.

I had to call the boys to help me and it took us quite a while to convince him to go back inside the house. He did this many times and we had to be watchful for him.

But he kept saying, "I wanna go home."

No matter how many times I asked him to say where is the home you want to go to, he didn't answer me. He simply said it every day. There were times when I heard him calling, "Mummy!" but because he normally called me Mummy, I would answer. Eventually I noticed that when I was beside him, he still called out Mummy, and I sensed that he was not calling me. A few times, he said, "They are here."

I did not like this unusual change in Ven but I kept it to myself. I was working out what to do when Otis sent us the money for our plane tickets. We were in a situation again where we did not have money for Ven's dialysis. I emailed Ven's cousin Everton in Springfield, Virginia in America, and he was very helpful. I explained everything to him, and we spoke on the phone and Everton gave me very encouraging words and he sent me money straight away for Ven's dialysis.

Another person who was really supportive and helpful to me at this moment was Aunty Adelfa Barros. She asked me to take her 18 carat gold ring to the pawn shop and pawn it to use the money for Ven's dialysis. My friend Yvonne in the UK also helped me with money towards the dialysis, and so did one of Ven's cousin's daughters in Jamaica. My friend Mark also sent me money, but

Chapter 15 - The Philippines; spirits, miracles, Typhoon Sendong

I still had to go to the head of the hospital to ask him to sign a permission paper each time for the dialysis because I still wasn't able to pay the outstanding balance I owed the hospital.

At this time, my brother Jorge and his wife Richel moved back in to live with us. I helped them to forgive each other and resolve their marriage problems. Pastor Noel helped Jorge find work and our lives settled into a regular routine together. I finished packing the things we needed to take to England and sold everything we could sell. But one day, my father Luis was very ill and had to be admitted to the same hospital Ven attended. He was there for more than a week and every day there was medicine to buy and different check-ups, then even more medicine. It was more struggle for me because my family did not have anything to contribute to buy his medicine. This time, I was attending two patients I needed to find money for. It was a very tough position to be in, physically, mentally, emotionally and, most of all, financially.

Meanwhile, Ven was at home needing care, having dialysis twice a week plus his tablets. We had to take it in turn to be in the hospital to look after my father. The doctors and nurses came and gave them medicine but we did the rest for our patients, making sure they ate on time, feeding them, washing and changing them, and so on. When Ven was in the hospital for his dialysis treatment that week, I had to run to and from where he and my father were. We had no money again and I had to ask Aunty Adelfa again for help. My niece came to buy some of my father's medicine. It was very tough when it was my turn to watch him. We had to hold him because, like Ven, he wanted to get out of the hospital. I could not sleep because I needed to attend to him all night long. In the morning, I had to find money in preparation for Ven's next dialysis.

I went to see Sister Norma, who had money for me for the dialysis the next day and also for the public transport to take us to the hospital. It was also very good that JJ was always there now he had finished school because I needed him to get his dad to his wheelchair after I changed his clothes every time we take him to his dialysis. Although Ven was able to walk a few steps, he needed to be watched because he could easily fall.

In November 2011, Ven was struggling to breathe again and, as usual, we rushed him to the hospital. We were in the emergency department; the place was packed that morning, as usual. They placed Ven in one of their beds and I saw four people die in an hour while we were there. I was very worried about Ven, who was very restless, and we had to hold him and watch that he did not get up and walk out. The next day, he was transferred to a room where there were four patients. He had to get the usual injection to reduce his blood pressure, and this cost me a thousand pesos per injection. At the same time, he had to go for his normal dialysis treatment. I went home, locked myself in toilet and cried! I smoked a lot that day! However, the song *You Raise Me Up* was playing again in the background and it really helped me to carry on! I found the strength to ask God where I can go next to get more money for all these problems that I had to solve. I decided the only person I could ask again was Everton in America and, of course, he sent me the money immediately. He was amazing!

Ven was in the hospital for a couple of weeks this time. I had to ask the head to sign another promissory note again because I still had an outstanding hospital bill to pay. We had to take Ven home because he was so restless. If the head wouldn't sign the paper to discharge Ven, the doctors wouldn't send him home. I went to see Sister Norma from the church and she said Pastor Noel would have a word with the head of the hospital to ask if they could discharge Ven, which they did. Later on, I was told the head of the hospital was a Christian; he gave an order to give us free blood for Ven every time he was due to go on dialysis and that was great!

Chapter 15 - The Philippines; spirits, miracles, Typhoon Sendong

Coming out from the hospital that evening, I forgot that it was my birthday. When we arrived home, the house was dark inside; it looked as though no one was home. I opened the door and, when I switched on the light, my family were all there singing "Happy Birthday." They had contributed money and cooked a meal for us, and bought me a birthday cake and drinks. I was very touched and there was karaoke singing, which we all enjoyed. After feeding Ven, I took him to bed and I joined the family to sing different songs. One of the songs was entitled *You're the One*. I remembered when Ven and I were sending recorded tapes to each other. I sang this song to him in one of my tapes, just for him. As I sang the song on this occasion, I was in tears because I remembered and felt the same feeling when I sang it for Ven all those years ago.

That week, I received another email from Otis asking me to confirm when we were coming back to England. I was very excited, but also very disturbed. I did not know how to go about it. I knew that we owed a lot of money to the hospital and it was not a very straightforward thing to do to leave the country. I had to sort things out and I had people to see. We could not go anywhere without money. I told Ven we were getting things ready to go back to England. We had photos taken with the family. I asked the hospital about the procedure we needed to follow to take Ven back to England in his condition and how to get the doctor's permission. I was happy going into the hospital and was focused on going back to England. I was ready to make promises to everyone we owed money to, including the hospital.

However, I was very disappointed when I was told I needed to pay the full outstanding balance, and that when Ven had his next dialysis, the balance would go back to zero, otherwise there would be no treatment for him. I did not know what to do. I had to pay 26,000 pesos as well as, on top of that, I had creditors giving me final notices with more interest to pay if I did not pay the overdue amount I owed. I had run out of people to call on.

153

In the end, I decided to use some of the money for our plane ticket. Ven needed to have his dialysis the next day so I paid the outstanding balance. I was very sad when my family was talking to me about how happy they were that at last we were going back to England; my heart felt very sad and I was very concerned about what to do now. I did not tell anyone about it.

On December 16th 2011, we came home in the night from Ven's dialysis. When Ven was in bed, JJ and I stayed up very late and watched films together. JJ went out to the shop and bought some sweets. It had been raining heavily the whole day. JJ saw my niece's dog and other dogs in the neighbourhood crying out, looking up at the sky and wanting to climb into the house. JJ ignored them and came back in, and we continued to watch the movie.

At 1:30am, December 17th 2011, we could hear many people shouting outside. JJ opened the door to see what was happening. But, before we knew it, the door was smashed wide open by the water from the flood outside. When the door was forced open, we saw the water on top of the wide open door coming right into the house. It happened so quickly, I shouted, "JJ, put Daddy on your back and run upstairs!"

I went to the wardrobe and grabbed the folder where I kept Ven's medical records and our passports, and I grabbed my shoulder bag. The water was climbing up so fast, higher and higher. People were everywhere, shouting for help! We were on the second floor and most people were climbing up to join us, children and adults, and also a neighbour who had recently come out of the hospital after a major operation. She was taken upstairs in our house and she was in terrible pain, but saving her life was more important than the pain she was suffering. Everyone was screaming, crying, calling their children's names. Fortunately, Jorge and Richel, who were still living with us, were already upstairs.

Chapter 15 - The Philippines; spirits, miracles, Typhoon Sendong

It was a very scary experience we all went through that night. We cried and asked our God to help us. I was screaming and saying, "Lord, save us from this."

Everyone continued to cry and scream because they were so frightened! I said to everyone, "Stop crying, we need to pray to God!" and they prayed with me.

Jorge cried out to the Lord to save us. He said, "We still want to live, forgive us from our sins. I will be a changed person if you save us from this."

I was now talking too and asking God, "Lord, are we going to die now?" Then, in a few seconds, I remembered my circumstances and the struggles I was going through, and I thought that perhaps it would be good to die now; we had struggled so much! I said, "This is the end, isn't it, Lord? That was it!" Then, standing in JJ's bedroom upstairs, I embraced Ven and JJ and said, "Darling, this is the end of our lives, we are all going to die now."

At that moment, I was convinced we were going to die in that house. There were many of us there, about 20 people, including the children. After hugging Ven and JJ, we came out of the bedroom and I kept praying, "Lord, forgive us all our sins. If you want to take us all tonight, please take us all home to you, our Father. We surrender our lives to you right now."

And, at that moment, suddenly I felt and heard my thoughts saying, "No, you are not going to die! You are all going to live." I felt it very strongly in my heart. At the same time, I saw the water continuing to rise up so fast that it was very scary to look at! I remember lifting up my right hand and looking at the water. I said, "In the name of Jesus! Stop! You do not climb up, you go down."

I felt I had the authority to talk to the water.

At that moment, we noticed that the water did not continue rising up! All of us were very happy and someone screamed, "The water has stopped rising!"

But Jorge shouted, "I don't trust the water. We all need to climb up to the roof. And we need to do it now!"

So we did. The men made something for us to use to climb up. JJ and the men helped Ven climb up to the roof. The rain was still pouring heavily. We were all soaking wet up there, but we felt safer. We managed to gather together sitting on the middle part of the roof, lining up from end to end. JJ was with Ven at one end and I could not get to them because it was not easy to move around, so I stayed where I was. JJ made sure his dad was sitting comfortably and he was holding him with his cousins. Ven kept on calling, "Mummy!"

I called back and reassured him that I was fine, that he had JJ and he needed to sit still because he might fall. I told him to hold onto JJ and he did.

We were all screaming for help to the rescuers on the helicopters but they did not come for us because it was very dark and the water was very high. Ven, in his very weak voice, was also screaming for help! It made me cry to hear his frail voice shouting for help. I was very concerned about us falling off because the roof was very slippery. We had to sit still and not make a lot of movement. My niece KC and nephew Rhyme were with us and they called to their mum from the other house. They had also climbed to the top of the roof and we were glad when they answered us. I thanked God we were safe and had not lost anybody in our area. Certainly God was with us that night.

We were on the roof until 8am the next day. When daylight came, it was a great feeling to see the water going down. We came off the roof slowly, one by one, using the small piece of

Chapter 15 - The Philippines; spirits, miracles, Typhoon Sendong

wood we had used to climb up. The water by this time was up to our legs. Everyone in our neighbourhood was very happy; no one in our neighbourhood had died. Our house was badly damaged and lots of houses were swept away by the flood, including houses belonging to my family. Rescuers came to direct us where to go. One of them placed Ven on his back and walked him to the Barangay Hall in Macasandig. They reached the hall before us, but my nieces and nephews were there to take care of Ven. Walking from the house to the main road barefoot, we saw a lot of dead bodies because the rescuers had lined them up on the side of the road. It was very devastating! There were plenty of people who had died; most of them were found in their homes with their children. They were stuck in their homes and could not run to save their lives.

When we reached the Barangay Hall, Ven was there with our relatives. We felt very hungry but we did not have any food to eat. I left Ven with the family, and JJ and I went to find food for all of us. We were still soaking wet and walking barefoot. No vehicles could come to the area. The whole place was badly damaged where we lived. The Barangay Hall was so packed with people, they had to find another place to bring the other victims from that disaster.

We had been hit by Typhoon Sendong, which was declared the world's deadliest storm in 2011. A National State of Calamity was declared and almost 50,000 people lost their homes, 13 areas were affected and 1,000 people died. Many victims were crying and screaming because they had lost their loved ones, and many more of them were missing. People I knew who lived next to our area had died. Some of my relatives on the other side of the city had died with their families. That morning, I was very glad when I discovered that my sisters Nellie and Jennelisa and their families were alive. They were all crying and thanking God that morning.

When JJ and I got to the food shop, there was a very long queue. Although there was help from other sources, there were more flood victims than helpers. They used most of the local schools to house the homeless people. We stayed in the hall that whole day. Jorge and Richel went back to the house to find what they could take and made sure there was someone there. The local thieves liked it when there was a disaster because they stole what they liked. In fact, most of the thieves pretended to be helpers but they looted the homes they helped! Jorge and Richel had to put our door back in so they could close and lock it behind them. I was blessed that Jorge and Richel were with us because I could not have sorted these things out on top of our present situation.

It was getting late at night and I was wondering where we could go where Ven could lie down and rest because there was nowhere to lie down in the hall. Later that evening, my brother Joe Marie came. We ate together with the supplied food for the victims. After we ate, Joe Marie said he would take us to his little home where at least Ven could lie down. He put Ven on his back and we started to walk. At that moment, Jorge and Richel appeared. They were surprised we were going to take Ven to Joe Marie's home because he lived in a hilly place, a long walk from the main road, and it was not easy to get there with Ven. Jorge suggested we go to the church and rest Ven there.

When we arrived at the church, Pastor Noel was very glad to see us. He said they had been looking for us all day. He had already booked a hotel for the victims that he knew and he took us there.

I had a terrible asthma attack in the night. I could hardly breathe. I had lost my voice because of all the screaming I had done the night before. I could only whisper. Pastor Noel gave us food and drinks in the hotel, and made sure we were dry and rested. I was concerned about Ven because we had lost his tablets. I needed to go to the hospital to get his prescriptions. The next day, my niece KC found my phone, which I had dropped in the house while

Chapter 15 - The Philippines; spirits, miracles, Typhoon Sendong

we were praying the night before. She dried the phone, charged the battery and made it work again. That was how I managed to contact Helen. Dear Helen gave us money that day.

Pastor Noel came to visit us the next day and told us they were looking for a place for us to move into. Four days after the flood, in the hotel where Pastor Noel had placed us in, my phone rang. It was our friend Roger from England. He was very happy he got me on the phone. He had been searching on Facebook and messaging and calling me since he heard about the flood on the international news. They were very worried about us. I was still struggling to talk. I was whispering but working hard to explain to Roger what had happened and what our situation was.

He said to me, "Listen! Work out how much you need to pay the hospital and your other debts, and come back to England as fast as you can. I will send you the money you need. Do it as quickly as possible. Email me and I will book flights for the three of you to fly to England."

I could not believe what I had heard! My mind was blank and I was struggling to breathe. I could hardly speak, but I managed to say in a whisper, "Thank you, Roger!"

He said, "Do it as soon as possible. Email me how much you need and when I can book your flights."

The moment I put the phone down, I forgot about my asthma; I was very glad to think of us back in England at last.

The hope came alive inside me again!

You raise me up by Leila Wilks

Chapter 16 - From the Philippines to London; Ven goes home at last

Otis had communicated with Roger after the flood and was helping me to know how to deal with the doctor, whose signature we needed to approve Ven's travel on the plane. I continued trying to get the doctor to sign the papers, allowing Ven to travel. I went to three different hospitals and one clinic. That was a big challenge for me because Ven's doctor told me plainly he was not going to sign it because Ven was not allowed to fly in his condition.

Glory found us a place to live but when we got there, it smelt strongly of paint as it was a newly decorated house, and because of Ven's condition and my asthma, we could not stay there. Pastor Noel found us an apartment near the church behind Cogon Market. We had stairs to climb but it was a nice, comfortable place for us to stay until we left the country.

Although it was a great feeling to know we were going to fly back to England, I still had many things to sort out. I continued to use the money Otis sent us for Ven's twice weekly dialysis. Ven was fine because he had the treatment on time and regularly. He was also taking his maintenance tablets on a regular basis. It was a great feeling when every time we took him to dialysis, I had that money in my hand and still had money for further dialysis until we left the country. I had explained to Ven what was going on all the way through the process; what I was doing and what was happening. When I said to him, "We are going back to England for the treatment you need and you will get back to normal health and we will start our life again," he smiled. I could see the happiness in him. His eyes smiled and he nodded his head.

161

In the apartment where we stayed our last few weeks in December 2011, before leaving the country, I had a comfortable and less stressful life. On Christmas Day, however, I remember receiving so much food and many drinks and clothes from the people in the church and from other countries helping the typhoon victims. Every day, we went to our damaged home and sorted out what was left that we still could use. Jorge and Richel were doing most of this for us. They did so much cleaning up and they sorted out the things we could take with us from the things I had packed before the flood. Most of the clothes were damaged and we had to throw them away. JJ and I repacked two suitcases but most of the clothes we wore had been given to us. These did not fit us well and were too loose or too tight. We had lost everything and it was devastating to look around at how damaged the place was and the surrounding areas. We had to wear long boots to avoid catching diseases from the water. There were a few rich people who lived further down from our area, but during that time we were all equal because we were all victims of that flood disaster.

In my country, there is no middle class, you are either rich or poor. The majority of rich people do not mix with poor people unless the poor people are working for them. Although, of course there are few who are different and have a heart of gold, such as Glory and Roly Tan, and the church family.

Roger had booked our flight this time, and we were leaving from Manila Airport on the December 31st 2011. I started to panic because Ven's doctor was hiding from me and still refused to sign the permission to travel paperwork. He did not want to sign the documents. He already told me the previous month that Ven was not in a position to travel on the plane. I knew the risk, but taking Ven home to England was his wish and it was very important for us to get back to England to give Ven the proper treatment he needed. However, one day one of the nurses, who was very helpful and attentive to Ven, told me the doctor was in

Chapter 16 - From the Philippines to London; Ven goes home at last

the emergency room. I went there quickly but the doctor was not happy to see me.

I said to him, "I understand the risk, but you signing this form is our only hope to go back to the UK. It is Ven's request."

He took a pen and signed. I was very happy! I thanked him and said, "Goodbye."

I rushed home because we only had two days left to get everything ready. JJ was very sad saying goodbye to his friends. We had arranged Ven to have his last dialysis the day before we left. The night before we left, JJ went to see Pastor Noel, who gave him a Bible and one for me as well. My family stayed with us on our last night and they travelled with us to the airport to see us off.

At six o'clock in the morning, Glory picked us up and she gave me more clothes and a pair of sandals to wear. Ven's trousers that day were very loose. We could not find clothes that fitted him but we did not think it mattered. I gave Ven his medication before we left and he could not wait to get on the plane.

I was very touched at how much Glory helped us. I gave her a big hug and thanked her. She was happy to see us go but said she would miss us. We reached Manila Airport and my nephew Randy met us there. We had something to eat in a small restaurant while waiting to board the plane. I was very happy at that moment, and so was Ven and JJ. We were all excited to get on the plane. JJ was walking with his dad, holding him up.

Our stopover was in Singapore. We were there for more than three hours, sitting in the waiting room. I gave Ven something to eat and drink. Ven looked fine. I was watching him all the time, giving him his tablets after food. We then boarded the plane for London Heathrow. We put Ven in between us; he was smiling, looking at JJ and I, and nodding his head; he was very relaxed.

He wanted to eat everything he was given on the plane and he enjoyed his cup of tea. Ven asked to go to the toilet a few times. One time I was a bit embarrassed because his trousers fell off on the floor. We watched films together on the plane. JJ found a nice song from the music station and held the headphones to his dad's head and Ven was listening to it, nodding his head and smiling.

Halfway through the journey from Singapore, Ven told me his head was hurting. I gave him the liquid medicine the doctor normally gave him while he was on dialysis, to bring his blood pressure down. Ven was crying. I reassured him that we would soon arrive in Heathrow Airport and he needed to stay strong! I had to control myself not to panic, and slowly I rubbed his head and eventually he fell asleep. I was very relieved to see him sleeping. I prayed to God to help us arrive in London without any problems.

My heart was jumping in happiness and joy when the plane landed at Heathrow Airport! Ven was very happy too, smiling and nodding his head. We placed him on a wheelchair and pushed him to the exit. But I noticed Ven's nose had blood on it. I wiped it away and JJ held him and walked towards the taxi area. I rung Mark and told him we did not have any money for a taxi so he came to pick us up.

I was very glad Mark had offered us his house to stay in until the caravan was available. I remember chatting to Mark in the car while he was driving and looking around at the beauty of the places we passed. Everything for me that day was beautiful. I was very glad to be back in England and Ven was going to be fine. When we got to Mark's home, he had already prepared his room for us. I asked Ven if he wanted a cup of tea, and he said, "Yes, please!"

He was sitting on the edge of the bed, but while I was away, he fell off. I called JJ and we helped him up while Mark called the

Chapter 16 - From the Philippines to London; Ven goes home at last

ambulance. At that moment, Otis arrived, in time to carry his dad from the fall. The ambulance arrived and the medics asked us so many questions. They talked to Ven but he did not answer. They placed him on the floor and put an oxygen mask on him. His blood pressure was very high as they drove him to hospital. I felt that day was the longest day of my life. In the emergency room, the doctor asked about all the medication that Ven was taking. The doctor took us to a private room and asked if I would like them to carry out resuscitation on Ven. They said if he survived, his body would be damaged.

I said, "Yes, please do it. We want him to live."

I started to feel really scared! I had not expected this! He looked fine when we arrived in the morning. In fact, he had been walking around Mark's house. I had such a big hope that his health would improve when we got back to England because he would get proper and regular treatment.

Late in the afternoon, the doctor told us to say anything we wanted to say to Ven because even though he could not respond, he would hear us. In that moment, I still had a hope of him recovering and I was talking to him, encouraging him to fight and come out of it. I told him he was a winner and he never gave up on us. Then JJ talked to him, and so did Otis. I was still hopeful he was going to survive. I did not see him dying. Later, Roger and Paula arrived, and so did other friends, including Mel, Ven's ex-wife.

The doctors were checking Ven's heartbeat every few minutes. Suddenly, Ven's breathing became much louder as if he was snoring. It went on for a long time. They checked his heartbeat again and I heard a big breath being released from him. After that, the doctors asked everyone to leave the room. We saw the doctors and nursing staff trying to resuscitate Ven, but at 9:30pm January 1st 2012, the doctor came out of the room and told us Ven had died.

You raise me up by Leila Wilks

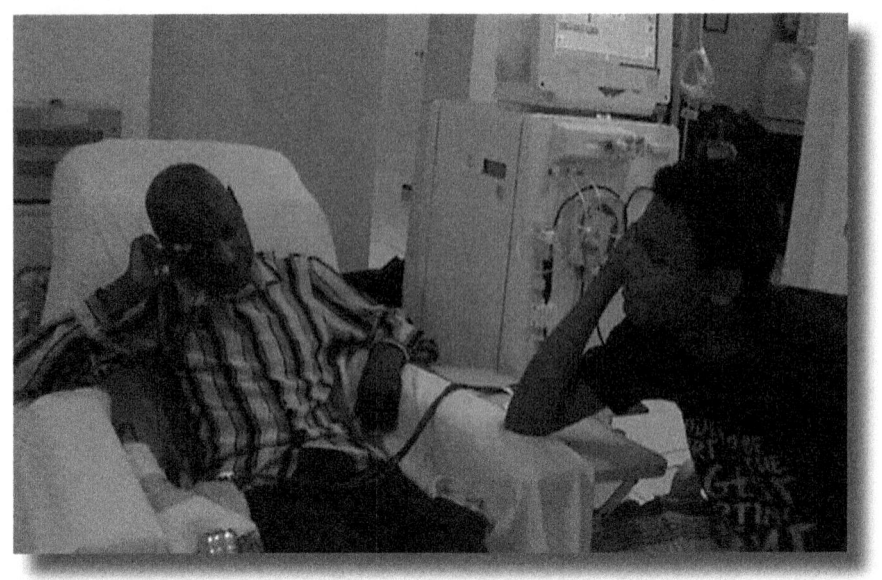

Ven and JJ during one of his dialysis treatments

JJ and I, a few months after losing Ven in 2012

Chapter 17 - London; reality, relatives and reading

Writing this book in my bedroom in our flat in Hertfordshire, where JJ and I live now, I have had to stop many times to cry. I feel the same as I felt on the night Ven died. It is a very painful feeling. I struggle to continue to write. But I pray to God He will give me the courage and strength to finish this book because it is not about me, it is about the people who can learn from my story and be encouraged by it. My reason to live now is for my JJ, and to help other people and my family back home in the Philippines.

On the night Ven died, reality hit me! I had lost everything. I screamed like a hopeless, little child. I could not believe he was dead. I sat there next to him, calling him, crying and screaming, trying to wake him up! I had lost hope and happiness completely! I did not remember about our son JJ. He was behind me trying to be strong and comforting me. I was lost! The pain of knowing that Ven was gone forever was unacceptable! I looked at Roger and Paula, and said to them, "He is gone!" I felt I wanted everything to finish that night. I wanted to stop living. I was so tired. Mel started to pray over me and eventually I calmed down and simply sobbed and sobbed.

We went back to Mark's home that night. Coming out of the hospital, I felt the whole world fall on top of me. I felt very heavy. I continued sobbing in Mark's home all night long. In the morning, I called Pastor Noel in the Philippines and told him Ven was gone. He prayed on the phone for me. I cried with him. I rang Ven's cousin Everton in America, who had helped us so much financially. JJ sent messages on Facebook about his dad passing away. I started to receive calls from our friends and Ven's family.

My mind was completely blank and I did not know what to think. I went through the flow of what to do, helped and supported by Otis, who conducted all the official processes and dealt with the hospital. Otis also planned Ven's funeral. He took more days leave than he was entitled to. His planning and scheduling for the funeral was so intense because of the limited days of leave he had. He was responsible for most of the arrangements on my behalf. I simply wanted to die too. I went out on the street and intentionally walked in the middle of the road hoping the drivers would hit me. JJ rescued me. I was very glad JJ was so strong for me. He was always there near me. He did not want me to go out on my own. My mind was hoping I would die now so Ven and I could be together. I thank God that He held JJ up. Even though he was suffering deep inside as well, he was able to be there and continued to be strong for me.

The second night after Ven's death, I cried almost all night.

I said to God, "What is next? I thought you would keep Ven alive for us. Me next Lord, take me! I want to die now. I do not want to carry on living. What's the use? I do not have anything. I don't want to live anymore. I have nothing left. There is no reason to continue to live. Take me, Lord!"

Because I was tired, I fell asleep saying these things.

But, suddenly, I was woken up by a slap on my lap! I got up and looked around me, but no one was there. A very strong silent message in my head commanded me to look at my son, who was sleeping in the room beside me. It said to me, he is the reason you have to live. I looked at JJ and reality hit me!

All I had been thinking and feeling was about me, and the pain of losing Ven, and what we had been through for the past few years. I stood there, watching my son, and realised I needed to carry on living for him. He needed me to guide him in his life

Chapter 17 - London; reality, relatives and reading

now, and encourage him. These thoughts and feelings helped me to survive.

Otis instructed JJ to help with the funeral arrangements, although he was struggling with losing his father too. Otis told me what I needed to do about Ven's pension and helped us find a coffin, even though we had such limited money. Mel, Otis's mum, was a great help to me as well because she paid for Ven's funeral, although I was able to pay her back later that same year. I felt as if life had stopped to function for me, but I had to go to the funeral director and answer their questions. JJ and I had arranged to see Ven's body in the funeral home. Mark drove us there. When I saw Ven lying down on that bed, he looked as if he was sleeping and I wanted to talk to him, but I knew in my heart it was useless to talk to him because he would not hear me anymore. It was only his body, not him. The pain started to torture me while I looked at him. We did not stay long.

JJ and I started to get to know the place where we were staying. Mark told us there was a lake nearby plus a big park where people played football. We went there. I sat and smoked and cried while JJ played football. Together, we walked to the town and found a methodist church. I remembered on the day of our baptism in the Philippines, Pastor Noel had told me to find a church that taught a lot about the Bible. JJ and I went into the church and I asked a lady if it was possible to talk to the Pastor. I told her that my husband had died a few days ago. She asked JJ and I to sit in a little room and very soon a Pastor came into the room. I told him what had happened to us. He was very compassionate and he prayed for us before driving us back to Mark's house.

Otis went to the place where we were going to bury Ven, took a photo and showed it to me. He provided a coat for his brother because JJ did not have appropriate clothes to wear. On the day of Ven's funeral, Otis hired a car to help us move all our things to live with him in Hemel Hempstead.

You raise me up by Leila Wilks

The funeral was arranged on January 17th 2012, in Herongate Wood Cemetery in Brentwood, Essex. Roger and Paula, thoughtful as ever, bought me a suit and shoes to wear to the funeral. They also gave us money to have a hair cut each. They had given us most things we needed, including coats and jackets, food and toiletries, as did Otis too. Mel and Otis' uncle Mike took us to the shopping centre and bought JJ a suit and a pair of shoes to wear for the funeral. Everyone around us at this moment was doing everything they could for us to help us to cope and function. My mind was blank! I could not think straight. I did not have any desire to do anything. I felt there was no tomorrow for JJ and I. I was not worried. I felt numb and empty.

The first Sunday after Ven's death, JJ and I went to church, where the Bible reading that day felt as if God had sent these words especially for us.

> *"He gives power to the weak and to those who have no might.*
> *He increases strength. But those who wait on the Lord shall renew*
> *their strength. They shall mount up with wings like eagles. They shall*
> *run and not be weary, they shall walk and not faint."*
> ***Isaiah 40:29:31 NKJV***

I received phone call after phone call. People feeling sorry for us and saying their condolences on the phone. Someone said, "Whenever you need help, please ring me." It reminded me of the time in the Philippines when I was running around asking for financial help for Ven's next dialysis and I had sent messages to all our friends in England. This person was one who had not replied to my messages, to my cry for help then. This time, I was angry, and I said, "Ven is gone! I do not need help anymore!"

It was annoying to think that when Ven was still alive and desperately needed help, there were not many people who actually sent help. Now, many people wanted to talk to me and try to encourage me, but deep in my heart I knew no encouragement

Chapter 17 - London; reality, relatives and reading

could help me. All I knew was I had to live for JJ. Through all of this, the couple who really helped the most was Roger and Paula. They were always there for us. They genuinely believe that we help and look after other people when they are alive because when they are dead, there is no need. They believe in caring for family and friends. Without the love, care and support of Roger and Paula, we would not be here now. They are friends and family to us. They were sent by God to us, and I do not say that lightly. They know what we went through in life, and they have helped JJ and I to move on. With God's help and guidance, everything is possible.

The day of Ven's funeral arrived. Roger, Paula and Mike, Roger's brother, arrived at the house. I cried and hugged Mike. I remembered the last time Ven and Mike had seen each other. It had been in a business seminar and they had enjoyed a good laugh together about something.

Otis arrived, and we were ready to go. He made sure everyone was ready to read their tributes. The limousine with the coffin arrived. As soon as I saw the coffin, I started crying again! My heart was aching looking at the coffin, but we got in the other limousine behind it. I remember it was very painful to look at the coffin in front of us and be reminded that Ven was gone forever.

When we arrived at the church, people started to come and show their sympathy to us. In times of distress, however, people rarely remember what is said. What they most remember is who was there. Familiar faces offer strength beyond description. They provide comfort for the deep feelings of loneliness setting in from the loss. The gift of presence is one we are all capable of offering, even if we are tongue-tied and uncomfortable.

I felt nothing but sorrow and pain that day. Going inside the church following the coffin was very painful. I could not stop crying! All I can remember was Roger and Paula always there next to JJ and I. We were supposed to celebrate Ven's life, but I couldn't; the pain of losing him was overwhelming. Otis delivered the opening remarks himself, and I don't know how he did it. Paula read my tribute for me; I could not do it. JJ read his tribute about his dad. He was strong and I admired his and Otis' courage. While the Bishop was preaching, my mind was empty, I could hardly think for myself. Soon enough, the service has finished and, one by one, people went to the coffin to look at Ven's body.

JJ and I got up and looked at his dad. I thought, is this what life is? And now it is finished? We started our journey to the cemetery. It was hard to think that we were about to bury Ven and that was it.

We arrived at Herongate Wood Cemetery and it was very painful to see the coffin going down into the hole in the ground. I wanted to go down as well, to be buried with him. I could feel JJ holding me tight. I was screaming as loud as I could, calling Ven! I could not cope seeing the coffin when they started to cover it with earth. I felt as if I wanted to pass out. Otis conducted the service and prayers, and I don't know how he managed to do it.

Afterwards, we went to a hall where they served food and drinks. Mel was helping with her sister and their families. Mark was there all the time, waiting to drive us back to his house to pick up our cases. He was very sad when we left. We had a long drive to where Otis lived and we arrived late in that same, sad night. His place was very comfortable and we had all the space and time we needed there to grieve.

My mind was still blank and I continued to cry in my room there. I could not sleep. I realised how important it is to enjoy life with our loved ones while they are still with us, because when the time comes that they are no longer with us, those moments we have with them are very precious indeed. Although we sometimes

Chapter 17 - London; reality, relatives and reading

annoy each other and argue with each other, those moments are not remembered when they are gone and misunderstandings do not matter anymore.

JJ and I talked about our happy memories with his dad. We laughed and cried together. It was a blessing from God that Otis took us to his apartment because the three of us grieved together. Every day when Otis came home from work, we talked about Ven and it helped us all.

JJ and I started to do the necessary things to settle in such as registering our names at the medical clinic and the library. It was nice to go to the library and have a couple of hours of free internet usage. It helped us to take our eyes off ourselves. We went to the nearest pond where we could see the ducks. JJ started to play football again and he continued to play his guitar. In the night, I heard him cry. I sat with him and we talked about it and cried together. It was the only thing we could do to release the pain in our chests. I had asked Otis where the nearest church was in the area. He showed me a couple of churches. One afternoon, I walked to one of the churches about 25 minutes away, but in my mind, I saw Ven everywhere I went. While I walked, I cried.

I remembered when we were building a business together in Woolwich and how we walked when we did not have a car. We enjoyed it and he liked to talk and meet people. It was a very painful experience walking on my own now, knowing he was not there anymore. In the first month after his death, I had people ringing me to find out how we were. But after that, only a few people rang, and it was always Roger and Paula and a few other people we were close to. The pain of losing Ven was tremendous and talking about him helped ease the pain.

JJ and I went to see a counsellor, but it did not help us so we tried several local churches. I missed Ven so much but I also knew I needed to do something for JJ and I to continue our life journey together now, without Ven. I needed to find a job and a place for us to live. I did not plan to stay with Otis for a long time. I was now trying my best to be strong for JJ.

I read my Bible every day and that took my mind away from thinking about Ven too much. I went to the library and borrowed books and CDs. I started to focus on reading again. Although I did not feel like doing anything because my mind was empty, reading helped stimulate my mind. I started to enjoy going to the library more and more, and I went every day. I discovered free courses I could take, including computer courses to learn how to use Microsoft, Excel and PowerPoint. I also found places that offered free employment support and help to put CVs together and apply for jobs online. I was told to contact someone called Jeremy Keeley, who ran an employment support programme, and at the same time JJ was getting help from a Youth Connection Programme. Otis helped JJ to write his CV and helped him deliver them to local shops, as well as coaching him about how to conduct himself in a job interview. Otis was being more like a father to JJ than a brother, and although he was very firm, it helped JJ. I prayed every day asking for God's guidance for us. JJ was called to an interview at a local shop called Wickes and on the day of the interview, he was very nervous. I talked to him, encouraged him and told him his daddy would want him to pass this job interview. I said, "Do it for Daddy. Think that Daddy is watching you."

When his name was called to go in to the interview room, he sent me a text and I sent him a reply, saying, "Do it for Daddy, man!" and I prayed for him at the same time. When he came home, he was amazed at how confident he was in his interview. Although he was nervous to start with, he came out feeling good about himself. After a few days, he received a letter offering him his first job and he was so excited. There had been ten of them interviewed, and only three were offered the job. I cried and thanked the Lord!

Chapter 17 - London; reality, relatives and reading

I continued with my job search and I looked up this man called Jeremy Keeley. He actually work quite close to where we were staying. I went to see him. I rung the doorbell of this big building, which he answered. He asked me to sit down and I explained to him I was new in the area and I had recently lost my husband. As soon as I said that, he asked me if I wanted to talk to the Pastor. I said, "A Pastor? Is this a church?"

He said, "Yes, as well as a community centre."

I was delighted, and said, "Yes, please! I would love to talk to the Pastor."

Jeremy went upstairs, and within a few minutes, Pastor Brian and his wife Dolly Boggis came down and introduced themselves to me. I felt as if I was in heaven. They asked me compassionate questions and I told them about Ven's death and the typhoon we had been through. I felt as if I was talking to my parents, telling them how I struggled and I needed to come home. In that moment, I felt I had found my home. I remember again the day when Pastor Noel baptised us in the Philippines; he had said to me, "When you go back to England, look for a church that really preaches the gospel." And here I was, with Pastor Brian and Dolly.

I didn't have a clue about many things, but I believe I was guided in their direction. Pastor Brian and Dolly walked me around the building, introducing me to everyone who was there. I felt very welcomed by everybody! I started crying and was not used to such caring attention. Pastor Brian and Dolly prepared a food bank voucher for me and Dolly showed me where to collect the bags of food. It was part of the church service to the community, helping people with no income to source food. I was amazed to see the amount of food in the shopping bags that Dolly and I were struggling to carry. Dolly walked with me to the place where we were staying. I phoned JJ and asked him to come downstairs to

175

help me carry all the food upstairs. I was very grateful to Pastor Brian and Dolly for their help on that first day I met them.

I was very excited telling JJ about my experience at the church and the community centre. To this day, I am still with Pastor Brian and Dolly. Here, I started to grow and have developed spiritually, mentally and emotionally. I have learned that to develop as a person, we need to be with people. We can't grow on our own. We are designed to be with other people. From that day, JJ and I have had many blessings from the Lord that we could never have imagined.

Chapter 18 - London to Hemel Hempstead; a life purpose at last!

I continue to read books, but the Bible is the greatest book ever written. It tells you how to live a blessed life. I joined South Hill Church, where they were running an Alpha Course, which I joined. I learnt so much about Christian life and our walk with the Lord. Every Sunday, I went to church and started to make friends there. I volunteered to help in the church being part of the welcome team, helping in the crèche and at different events they were running.

One day, when I was walking towards the town centre, I met a Filipino lady. She spoke my local language from back home and she asked me if I would like to work for her. She was desperately looking for someone to help her clean these big local houses once a week. I was glad to hear this and said, "Yes, of course. I'd love to help her."

She promised to collect me at 9am the next day and would drop me home after 5pm. Without any more questions, I accepted the job and I started to work for her, although I had never done house cleaning in England before. I did not have a clue about what to do, I simply wanted to earn money. She was willing to teach me, and I was willing to learn, but I was slow because I was scared of breaking the china ornaments and expensive possessions in the houses. The lady I was working for started to get very impatient with me and shouted at me as if I was a child! She forgot that I was much older than her, and she was very disrespectful. She worked fast and she was very demanding. I felt I would die from high blood pressure if I continued and I was really struggling with it. However, because I was desperate to earn money, I continued to work for her.

One day, I felt I needed to pray and ask God to help me to work faster without breaking things in the house. I also asked God to help me to cope with this lady's attitude. I was amazed because that day I worked faster than ever before. In fact, I finished what she asked me to do, and she was surprised too! This continued the following days and weeks, but it did not change her attitude towards me.

I shared this experience in our Alpha Course meeting that week. I was crying as I did this because I could not understand how someone from my own country could treat me the way she did. The following week I was with her, I felt stronger in my heart to tell her I wanted to stop working for her, and after she dropped me off, I told her.

Pastor Brian and Dolly told me there was a lady called Sandra who owned a cleaning company in our church and who might be looking for someone to help her. I met Sandra at a craft night in the South Hill Centre and she talked to me about the job. I was glad to know I would be working again. I worked with her to learn the job for one day and waited until she had a place available for me. Sandra was very helpful and sympathetic. Later on, we worked hard together, but it was interesting and fun. We grew together by sharing things with each other and it was amazing because I discovered that Sandra had several of my husband Ven's character. We developed a great friendship. There were ups and downs, but we learnt from each other.

I felt we had overstayed Otis' kind hospitality. I knew we needed to find our own home to live in so I started to walk around Hemel Hempstead looking for a home for us to rent. Pastor Brian and Dolly helped me, and they took me in their car to see several homes. It was quite hard for JJ and I because everything was new to us. In the past couple of years, our lives had revolved around hospitals, searching for help and looking after his dad. I prayed every day, asking God to help us find a home and settle down

Chapter 18 - London to Hemel Hempstead; a life purpose at last!

into our new life. Doing all these different things in the day had kept my mind away from thinking about Ven too much. But in the night, I had time to cry and think about him. At least in the day I was busy and my mind was occupied with new things to learn.

One morning, I had the idea to write down on a piece of paper a date when we were going to move to our new home. I stuck it next to the bathroom mirror and every time I looked at it, I prayed on it. I wrote, "10th May, we will move to our new home."

And it was amazing how God answered that prayer!

One afternoon, I was in my computer course when Sandra sent me a message saying a mum of her friend had a flat available to rent. I called Pastor Brian and we arranged to see the place together. When I saw the house number on this flat, I was happy because it was number 27, Ven's birth date. When we got into the flat, I looked around and I felt I was at home immediately. It was a very unusual feeling. I was 100% convinced this was the place for us.

Pastor Brian asked me, "Do you like it?"

"With a big yes," I replied.

It was funny because I forgot I did not have money to pay the deposit. I simply felt I wanted to move straight away without even worrying and thinking about the money. And I did not have any money at all! I was carried away with the fact that God had a plan for us and I left everything in His hands. When we talked to the owner, I was very glad to hear she did not ask for a deposit, but only one month's rent before we moved in.

I looked at Pastor Brian, and he said, "Are you sure you want this flat?"

"Yes," I responded.

He knew I did not have the money to pay for it, but he and Dolly signed the papers as a reference and guarantor for me and reassured the owner I would be able to afford it. We arranged the date to move in after Pastor explained my situation to the owner. I did not speak much because I knew JJ and I did not have any money. Pastor Brian dealt with everything on my behalf because JJ and I were new in the area. When we went back to the car, Pastor Brian told me that they would pay for the first month's rent. I was very happy indeed and I thanked God it did not cause me more stress and worry to get the place. The amazing thing was that the date we moved into our new home was May 10th! Pastor Brian and Dolly were also amazed at this and asked me to testify in front of the Sunday service in church.

The day we moved in was wonderfully unstressful. Everything we needed to move into our new home was provided for us from other people. I did not need to buy anything apart from a microwave. If I wrote down all the peoples' names who gave JJ and I possessions for our new home, the list would be very long. Our local church community also helped us move our things, using their cars to take us to our new home. I had never known a less stressful move than this. It was a great feeling to have a home again, especially after the typhoon and flood in the Philippines, when we had lost most of our few possessions.

It is a peaceful home that God has blessed JJ and I with. My bedroom window looks out to the trees and I can see birds there and hear them sing.

All my life, I believe I have been led to read books that I needed at that moment on my journey. For example, in Chris Palmer's book, *Living as a Spirit*, he discusses *The Hands of God's Divine Providence*. He says what makes our whole destiny a reachable possibility is the mercy and grace of God. Without these two

Chapter 18 - London to Hemel Hempstead; a life purpose at last!

endless attributes of God, we wouldn't be in a place to hear from Him. He says mercy and grace are two different concepts, which are often confused. Mercy is not receiving what we deserve. Grace is receiving what we don't deserve. Whether we are conscious of it or not, mercy and grace have been trailing us from the beginning of time, managing our destiny and upholding our future.

"Surely your goodness and love will follow me all the days of my life, and I will dwell in the house of the Lord forever."
Psalm 23:6

Mercy and grace are the stagehands working behind the scenes, directing the next path on our destiny. When mercy and grace manifest to assist us in this life and lead us into the fulfilment of our destiny, it is called divine providence. This is the ever-present, foreseeing care and guidance of God over His creation that directs us towards His ongoing purpose. After reading this book, I understood more clearly what had been happening in my life.

A week before my birthday, I was praying to God to teach me how to pray better. Anna Nicks had given me a gift and when I opened it, I cried because it was a book by Joyce Meyer called *The Power of Simple Prayer*. Again, my prayer was answered! In this book, I learned so much about the power of prayer and it gave me the urge to pray even more! I learned about petition and perseverance, intercession and agreement, the Word and the Spirit, the fourteen hindrances to answered prayer, and so much more.

I studied another book by Joyce Meyer, *Power Thoughts*, and I applied what I learnt from this book every day.

Even to this day, I use the twelve power thoughts, which Joyce teaches in this book. There are many books from which we can gather information about our journey with God, learning about His will and purposes for us. He is always with us.

Learning and applying what I learnt really helped me to grow and mature in Christ, and it helped me develop my strong faith in God. When the author Chris Palmer came to England in 2013, I went to the altar call where he laid hands on me and said God had sent me home to realign my life.

I now understand how it is not a coincidence that we meet people in our life. I can see now how God has provided JJ and me with the things we need to continue to live. And He has placed people in our lives to help us. All the people we have met, and friends who have helped us to survive our struggles, were part of our divine providence. It is an amazing fact that God never leaves us nor forsakes us, whether we feel near to Him or far from Him. Faith does not take any notice of feelings. Faith says you are complete in Him. It is not about how we feel, when we believe, everything is possible.

"He gives strength to the weary and increases the power of the weak. But those who hope in the Lord will renew their strength. They will soar on wings like eagles, they will run and not grow weary, they will walk and not be faint."
Isaiah 40:29:31

I live with this verse from the Bible, every day.

"A father to the fatherless, a defender of widows, is God in His holy dwelling. God sets the lonely in families, he leads out the prisoners with singing, but the rebellious live in a sun-scorched land."
Psalm 68:5-6

I believe in the importance of reading the word of God, to plant it in our hearts and when we need it, it is there. What we put in, is what we take out and more, because we will develop and

Chapter 18 - London to Hemel Hempstead; a life purpose at last!

become stronger as a person. My faith has developed through hearing and reading the word of God. I have learnt, there is nothing man can doubt if he learns to shout! It is hard to believe how I have changed completely. The woman who never wanted to be around other people and never say hello to a stranger. I used to enjoy my own company. It is amazing how some of my personality was blended with my husband's. I am still quiet when I need to be, but now I can be bold and open up to other people when I need to as well.

My heart's desire now is to continue to serve God.

After reading *The Purpose Driven Life* by Rick Warren, I discovered that my life purpose is to worship Christ with my heart, to serve Him with my shape, fellowship with His family, to grow like Him in character and to lead my family and other people to do the same.

God has placed strongly in my heart, the following Bible verse.

> *"The Spirit of the Lord God is upon Me*
> *because the Lord has anointed Me*
> *to preach good tidings to the poor.*
> *He has sent Me to heal the broken hearted,*
> *to proclaim liberty to the captives,*
> *and the opening of the prison to those who are bound."*
> **Isaiah 61:1 NKJV**

The Bible verse below describes what happened to me on my life journey.

> *"And we know that all things work together for good to those who love God, to those who are called according to His purpose."*
> **Romans 8:28 NKJV**

I felt God's calling to gather a group of women together to reach out to women who needed help and support. He wanted us to use our God given gifts and work together for the benefit of His church.

One day, Ven and my desire to build a children's home in the Philippines for the orphans and street kids will be fulfilled because I am going to do it. I know I can't build a home for all the children who don't have a home, and I can't take all the street children off the street, but I know I can do something about it. I can see myself doing it for the rest of my life.

I am very grateful to be a part of the Street Pastors Team in our town. God has placed me here, and I will follow His leading, wherever He wants me to go.

My journey is not finished yet. It will end when God takes me home. But I will end my story here. This is not the end, but a new beginning of our life journey. There are always trials and tribulations in life, but the way we respond to them will make the difference between failing and succeeding in this life. There are challenges I am facing to continue the journey on my own as a single parent to JJ, but God is with me. I know JJ sometimes feels he is going through changes that only his dad can help him with and that I cannot help him, but God will teach us the best way for us. He is a Father to the fatherless, and a defender of widows. I will continue to fight and I know God will not give me more than I can handle. When it is our hardest, we surrender it to Him, because on this stage, it is not our fight, it is His!

I encourage you all, if you have not known God in your life, to find someone that knows Him and listen to what they say about Him. God created us. Our job is to find our creator and develop a personal relationship with Him through Jesus Christ our Lord and Saviour. When we do this, our creator will help us find ourselves and we develop our inner self! Nothing changed

Chapter 18 - London to Hemel Hempstead; a life purpose at last!

in my life, until I started to have a personal relationship with our Lord and Saviour Jesus Christ.

In my past, I used to only pray when I was desperate, but I have discovered that whether we are happy or sad, it is important to pray and thank Him for being there for us as our Father. He is a friend who we can turn to when we need someone and He will carry us through the hardest times in our life. I am a living testimony that God will never leave us, nor forsake us; we only need to call on Him. The Bible refers to Jesus as a rock who never changes. He is the solid rock on which we can all build our lives. Jesus is the solid rock we can cling to when the storms of life blow and beat against us.

I hope to meet you one day in this journey of life. We all have a different journey to take, but we are secure when we travel with the Lord, knowing Jesus as our Lord and Saviour. Life is a choice. What we are now and where we are now is because of the choices we have made in the past. I could have made a choice to mix with people who like to go out to clubs and drink until they get drunk. I could have blamed anyone around us for our troubles. I could have blamed God. I could have blamed my parents because we were poor. I could have tried to kill myself again and again. I could have hated everyone in my life circle. But I decided not to do these things. Instead, I can see much better things in the future by making the right choices and following God's guidance and leading.

All the "I coulds" are actually things that would have taken me to hell and I would not see my husband again in eternity. By making the right choices, they will take me towards living life to the fullness and in the abundance that our Lord Jesus Christ has promised. I have claimed and live His promises. I felt free from the toxic feelings and thoughts I used to carry around wherever I went in the past. The feelings of being scared and useless, worthless and being worried about what people say or think about me. The feelings I experienced when I was a child in school, when I attended the flag ceremony, feeling nervous and almost passing out, because I thought everyone was watching me and I wanted to melt. All these feelings have died in me now, and I know I am a new creation in Christ Jesus.

> *"There is no fear in love, but perfect love casts out fear, because fear involves torment. But he who fears has not been made perfect in love.*
> **1 John 4:18 NKJV**

God is love. In His presence, there is no fear; it melts away!

Notes, Definitions & References

Notes

The names of Leila's family members are accurate, but the names of several people in her book have been changed to protect their individual identity.

At the time of publication, the Philippines currency of pesos were P10,000 to £200.

Definitions

- Marcos Government, page 17; Ferdinand Emmanuel Edralin Marcos, Sr. was the President of the Philippines 1965 to 1986 and ruled as a dictator under martial law from 1972 until 1981.

- Barangay Captain, page 17; highest elected official of a local administrative district.

- Guanabana leaves, page 133; fruit, also known as custard apple or soursop.

References

Pages 141 and 152, *You Raise Me Up*

The song was originally composed by Irish-Norwegian Secret Garden's Rolf Lovland and Brendan Graham. It was popularised by Josh Groban in 2003, then by the Irish band Westlife two years later, and is now sang as a contemporary hymn in church services.

Page 32-33, *Lift Up Your Hands*
Originally sung by Filipino Balladeer, Basil Valdez, before being popularised as a gospel song by Gary Valenciano.

Page 31-32, *Footprints in the Sand*
The original authorship of the poem is disputed, although most commonly attributed to Charles Haddon Spurgeon, 1880.

NKJV – The New King James Version is a translation of the Bible published by HarperCollins. The Testament was published in 1979, the Psalms in 1980 and the full Bible in 1982.

Leila's Five Life Principles

Faith

> *"Now, faith is confidence in what we hope for and assurance about what we do not see."*
> ***Hebrews 11:1(NIV)***

> *"But seek first His kingdom and His righteousness and all these things will be given to you as well."*
> ***Matthew 6:33(NIV)***

I used to apply first what I know and work hard towards it and when I struggle and am desperate for help, I turn to prayer. However, I have learnt that is not the right way; we are better to pray first. We think carefully about what we pass on to our children. But by the example of our lives, we can pass on to our children very important beliefs and behaviours; such as a good name or an honourable character. As you think about what you'll pass on to your children and grandchildren, never forget the example of your faith. The values we give our children are more important than the valuables we leave to them.

Family

We need our family's support when we are going through tough times. When I lost Ven, it was very reassuring to know I still had my son JJ with me, and he has me too. Hearing from my family in the Philippines, telling me how they loved and cared about me, also kept me going. Sometimes our family hurt us; I would encourage forgiveness here. When we do not forgive, we can destroy ourselves and ruin our future. We do not have to be with our family all the time, but to forgive is to release that toxic feeling inside you and leave everything to God. Ask God to help you to forgive. Many of us who say our families are important, don't live as if they are. They are important, but I believe we need to tell them how much we love and care about them, and we need to make time to spend with them. We do not want to leave it until we lose them and at their funeral say how much we loved them and all their qualities. I prefer to hear from my family now saying how much they love and care about me, because when God takes me home, I will not be there to hear it and feel good about what they say. After losing Ven, JJ and I had a family in England who were always there for us and we could telephone them anytime, even at one o'clock in the morning. Thank you, Roger and Paula, and Paula's mum, Tula. She treated me like her own daughter!

Finance

To be able to have money to buy our daily needs is important. If you are building a business, do everything you can to build it big. When we live not earning anything, it is not good for our confidence. I know sometimes we can't find a job, but if we continue looking and have a strong desire, we will find one and we will not stay long in that position. I was without a job for months and I did not feel good about myself. I have learnt when I earn money, that I need to have some put aside so that when crisis comes, I will have something to use. I have learnt from reading different books about how to manage our finances. Sometimes wisdom is learning from other people's experience.

Fitness

*"When we are young, we lose our health to develop our wealth.
When we are older, we lose our wealth to try to gain back our health."*
World Health Organization

We do not have to wait until we get old to look after ourselves. What we put in our body will come out somehow, or will develop something unpleasant. We need to eat healthy food and take food supplements if we are not getting the required daily nutrients our body needs. Regular exercise is also important. I know most of us are very busy, but we value our health and we need to make time to keep our body fit. We all know that to get fit, we need to exercise and have a healthy diet.

Friends
Jesus is my friend. He would never turn a friend away. When we truly value our friends, we always find the time to spend with them. I spend time with Jesus every day. Sure, we all need flesh and blood companions, but never overlook the reality of the Lord's presence. We can depend on it. With Him by our side, we are never alone.

Most of us have friends who are truly there for us. It is good to let them know how we appreciate them as our friend. Do not assume they know. We need friends when we go through struggles in life. When I lost Ven, it was meeting up with Roger and Paula and the family, Jenny Holder, and Yvonne Thompson, who kept JJ and I going. We talked about Ven and that helped me so much! It is more joyful to celebrate our success with true friends.

Life is clearer to me now, more meaningful, fruitful and joyful, now I am living my life with my best friend, Jesus!

> *"But seek first His kingdom and His righteousness and all these things will be given to you as well."*
> **Matthew 6:33**
> ***New International Version (NIV)***

My life passion is to help and encourage people who are suffering and hurting. I want to set up a home for the orphans and street kids in the Philippines, and to help them see there is hope for their future.

You raise me up by Leila Wilks

Acknowledgements

I thank all the key people God has placed in our lives. Without them, JJ and I would not be where we are now.

Roger and Paula Galloway, and their children, Jamie, Ian and Reece
Thank you for always being there to support, help and give us advice. All the things you have done for us will never be forgotten as long as we live. You made us a part of your family, and we are very blessed. JJ and I feel we are valued and respected by you all. Without you guys, we would never have got back to England and we would not have met new friends and our church family. You have helped me build my character and you are examples of great leaders. You have genuine hearts and want to see people develop and succeed. You have helped so many other people without expecting anything in return. This is the reason you are both blessed and prosperous. You believe in enjoying life and keeping the family together. You hold on to the belief that: *If you give a man a fish, you will feed him for a day, but if you teach him how to fish, you will feed him for a lifetime.* Your love for people, determination, hard work and perseverance has placed you where you are now in life. You both deserve recognition, great respect and love.

Pastor Noel Triviligio, Cecille, and their son TJ and daughter JT
Pastor, thank you for all the help and support from you and the City Alliance Church family in Cagayan de Oro City, Philippines. Without your continued help, we would not have been able to keep Ven on a regular dialysis machine and put food on our table. Pastor, you always encouraged me every time you led us to sing the gospel song, *Trust and Obey*, in our Sunday church service.

Glory and Roly Tan

Thank you so much for paying the rest of our big hospital bill. Without your help, we would have had to stay longer in the hospital and pay much more money. Also, thank you for giving us the groceries from your shop. My dear sister, Glory, you have a merciful heart.

Aunty Adelfa

Aunty, you pawned your ring a few times for me, so we could take Ven for dialysis. Thank you so much for your love, help and understanding.

Mark Pountain

Thank you, my friend, for being there for me. You sent us money several times for Ven's dialysis. I was very happy that, despite of what I went through, you were still there as a friend ready to help financially. Also, thank you for allowing us to stay in your home when we did not have a home to go to.

Everton Collins

Thank you so much for helping us financially and for your encouragement on the phone when things were very hard and I did not know where to go. I know you cared for your cousin Venroy so much. I will never forget how you helped us, even when we came back to England shortly after Ven had passed away.

To all my sisters and brothers: Enesia, Nellie, Jennelisa, Abel, Joe Marie, Jorge and Joel

Thank you so much for your moral support, love and help looking after Ven, when I was away sorting out other things and JJ was in school.

Acknowledgements

Bishop Otis V Wilks
Thank you so much for sending money to help us to come back before the flood happened and for keeping us for a few months in your apartment. We were homeless and you took us in and fed us. Thank you so much for everything you did for JJ and I. You played a big part in our journey and you brought us to Hemel Hempstead for God to continue His plan for us. You are part of the divine providence.

Melva Wilks
Thank you for the time we spent getting to know each other closer. You have a great heart for people, and you are special and a great sister in Christ. Thank you for all your help and love. You paid for your ex-husband's funeral; thank you for being so good to us when we needed help. You have demonstrated the love of Christ and the understanding that we are all children of God in heaven.

Jennifer Holder
Thank you so much for being such a family to JJ and I. You are a very unique person, very strong and determine. You are special, my dear sis.

Pastor Brian and Dolly Boggis
Thank you so much for everything you have done. Your support, help and prayers were badly needed. You are unique people and very special. Thank you for giving me a space to develop my God given gifts and ministry.

Sandra Satler
Thank you so much for giving me work and helping me in many different ways. You are a special sister in Christ, a prayer partner and a warrior! Thanks for listening to things that I have shared. We grew together in Christ and always had fun together. You are very special to me. In our challenging times, we both have learnt and benefited in a big way.

My prayer partners at South Hill Church, Hemel Hempstead
Abi Bankole, Tina Louise Khan, Sandra Satler, Dolly Boggis, Ify Onugha and Alison Graham. Thank you for backing me up in prayers.

Kelly Marie Dolling, Yvonne Thompson, and Folake Joy Egbeyemi
My friends who prayed with me, thank you.

Robin Oakes
Thank you so much for being very welcoming on my very first day in the church. You have helped and encouraged me to raise my hands in worship.

Sylvi
Thank you so much for all your warm hugs and kisses. For all the things you have given JJ and I. You are special, my dear sis.

Our Family Care Group leaders, Ross and Claire Crawley
Thank you so much for being a great family in Christ to JJ and I. You have blessed us so much! Thanks for your solid and determined attitude. You are always there ready to help.

To my anonymous family in Christ at the South Hill Church
You have kindly paid a big amount towards our debts. It has eased up the pressure on me in a big way. To the rest of my church family in South Hill Church, Hemel Hempstead, thank you with all my heart. I am sorry not to be able to write all your names here; it would make a very long list. You all have merciful hearts and are very active in giving. God has blessed JJ and I with you all. God has placed me in South Hill Church so I can serve Him to the fullness of my heart and I thank God for that.

Acknowledgements

Abiola Bankole
My dear friend and sister Abi, thank you so much for everything you have done for me. You are such an obedient child of God. You have a merciful heart and are steadfast. Your heart is set to support and encourage other people and stand in the gap. You are such a prayer warrior! To know a person well, is to be in their company often. I am very blessed to have known you. I thank God for you.

Mira Masters
Thank you so much for helping me to correct my written manuscript before handing it to my editor, Wendy. I appreciate the time you spent coming to my place and taking great effort to help with this important work.

I thank my friends, **a husband and wife in South Hill Church**, who bought me and JJ a brand new laptop when we moved in to our new home, and always checked up on us to make sure we were alright.

Thank you to **a friend in South Hill Church**, who came to pray for me a few times, shortly after we moved in to our new home. Your prayers helped me sleep well at night.

Doctor Maria Coutinho
Doctor Maria, thank you so much for everything you did for Ven and I during our time in Woolwich. I will never forget how you have helped me financially. You have done extraordinary things for us. You are such a unique, compassionate and thoughtful person.

Ruth Spooner
My swimming instructor. Thank you for your never-ending help and encouragement so I could learn to swim.

To my dear family in Christ in Kettering, Northamptonshire
Thank you so much for all the help you gave to JJ and I. You are a very unique and special family, and very determined to bring up your children in the way they should go. I always thank God for you.

My life mentors, through the books I have read on my journey, thank you.
Robert H. Schuller, Chris Palmer, Joyce Meyer, Kenneth Hagin, Smith Wiggles Worth, Wendy Alec, Rick Joyner, Rick Warren, Norman Vincent Peale, Florence Littauer, Mary K. Baxter, Dale Carnegie, Dwight Nichols, and many more.

My book coach and editor, Wendy Yorke, who believed in me and my story. Thank you so much for your patience and understanding working with me.

My publisher Chris Day, for your positive outlook and encouragement. Thank you; you too believed in me as an author, and believed in the value of my story. You have helped me so much to learn the things that I need as a new author. You are a wonderful person, very warm and thoughtful.

Acknowledgements